Social Sciences Research

Research, Writing, and Presentation Strategies for Students

Second Edition

Gail M. Staines
Katherine Johnson
Mark Bonacci

The Scarecrow Press, Inc.
Lanham, Maryland • Toronto • Plymouth, UK
2008

SCARECROW PRESS,

Published in the United States of America
by Scarecrow Press, Inc.
A wholly owned subsidiary of
The Rowman & Littlefield Publishing Group, Inc.
4501 Forbes Boulevard, Suite 200, Lanham, Maryland 20706
www.scarecrowpress.com

Estover Road
Plymouth PL6 7PY
United Kingdom

British Library Cataloguing in Publication Information Available

Library of Congress Cataloging-in-Publication Data

Staines, Gail M., 1961–
Social sciences research : research, writing, and presentation strategies for students / Gail M. Staines, Katherine Johnson, Mark Bonacci. — 2nd ed.
p. cm.
Includes bibliographical references and index.
ISBN-13: 978-0-8108-6024-7 (hardcover : alk. paper)
ISBN-10: 0-8108-6024-4 (hardcover : alk. paper)
ISBN-13: 978-0-8108-5665-3 (pbk. : alk. paper)
ISBN-10: 0-8108-5665-4 (pbk. : alk. paper)
1. Social sciences–Research–Methodology. 2. Social sciences–Study and teaching (Higher) I. Johnson, Katherine, 1958– II. Bonacci, Mark A. III. Title.
H62.S736 2008
300.72–dc22 2007023527

First edition by Gail M. Staines, Mark Bonacci, and Katherine Johnson, *Social Sciences Research: Writing Strategies for Students*, Scarecrow Press, Lanham, MD, 2000 ISBN 0-8108-3686-6 (cl) / 0-8108-3716-1 (pbk)

∞™ The paper used in this publication meets the minimum requirements of American National Standard for Information Sciences—Permanence of Paper for Printed Library Materials, ANSI/NISO Z39.48-1992.
Manufactured in the United States of America.

We dedicate this text to our past, present, and future students who struggle with these issues. We hope our instruction will help students in their educational careers.

Contents

Acknowledgments

We would like to thank the following for their input, their assistance with drafts, and their suggestions and revisions: David Staines, Don Luce, Victor Marwin, Marguerite Newton, Lillian Passanese, and Dr. Elizabeth Weston. We also must express our deep appreciation for grant assistance that helped produce a draft version of the first edition of this textbook. This assistance came from the Phi Delta Kappa National Honor Society and from the NCCC (Niagara County Community College) Foundation.

Our primary motivation to work on the first edition of this textbook, written from 1998 to 2000, came from our experiences teaching library research and scholarly writing methods at the community college level. After a collective thirty years of college teaching experience, we found that most first-year and many second-year community college students, as well as entering college and university freshmen, have not received instruction in areas in which they must rapidly become proficient to excel in upper-level social sciences courses. These areas include recognizing a scholarly source from a popular source; developing a logical, coherent, and sufficiently focused research question; conducting searches using electronic sources of information, such as the Internet and scholarly databases; and writing papers in an acceptable format.

What we have found is that many of the finer points of these endeavors cannot adequately be treated or reviewed in writing classes covering many other topics nor in social sciences courses already crammed full of essential material. Thus, this manual is designed as a resource for students, as well as their instructors, to help students succeed in carrying out library research in the social sciences, writing formal papers in the expected format, and orally presenting or defending such a paper. In addition, in this second edition, we have included more instruction on searches of information using electronic sources, such as the Internet, as well as new formatting guidelines that have been promulgated in the past 5 years.

The three of us, in addition to our colleagues, have spent numerous sessions in our classes, as well as in campus workshops, educating students on researching, writing, and presenting their library research papers. We thank all of our students, as well as those who attended and collaborated with us on these workshops.

Introduction

Students first entering 4-year colleges and universities, as well as at the community college level, are required to complete literature review papers based on scholarly research and writing. Today, students face computerized databases and "high-tech" literature searches that were unheard of even 20 years ago. *Social Sciences Research: Research, Writing, and Presentation Strategies for Students* is written to guide students through this process.

This manual is designed to give the reader step-by-step instructions for writing a social sciences literature review paper, which is also referred to as a research paper. Steps include formulating a research question, finding the scholarly literature necessary to help one treat or address this question, reading and understanding the literature, and actually constructing the paper and planning its oral defense. The process of forming an outline and then filling in this outline with the necessary data and details is also reviewed. Worksheets accompany each chapter, and a set of worksheets is published at the end of the book in Appendix C. Students may find that it is beneficial to supplement this manual with a book explaining social science research methods, such as Natalie L. Sproull's *Handbook of Research Methods: A Guide for Practitioners and Students in the Social Sciences*, second edition (1995).

The aim of this manual is to cover those elements of the scholarly research, writing, and presenting process that will help students become successful scholars of the social sciences and better informed critical thinkers and consumers in regards to published studies in the social sciences. We have also included four appendixes. Appendix A provides a list of research questions that have been posed by prior students. Appendix B is an example paper. Many of the examples used in the manual are either related to or taken from the example paper, such as the research question "Is violence in dating relationships conceptually distinct from violence in marital relationships?" Reference to the example paper provides a consistent theme throughout. Appendix C is the complete set of worksheets. Appendix D contains blank citation forms. These can be used to record references from books, chapters in books, scholarly articles, and Internet sites. Once completed, the forms can be cut and placed in alphabetical order. This expedites putting the information into correct format on a word processor.

This manual is written for you the student. As you are working through your research and writing, do not hesitate to ask your professors for guidance. Other places to find help on campus are in campus writing centers and, of course, in the library and via the library's website. You only need to ask for help.

1

Choosing an Appropriate Research Question

While high school instructors may have assigned topics for you to research and write on, most college courses will expect you to decide on a relevant topic or research question to write on. View this writing experience as an opportunity to fully use your creativity and explore your interests.

In choosing a topic to research, first remember that the topic has to hold enough interest for you personally so that you will write compellingly about it. Additionally, the topic should be of intrinsic interest to your target audience—the individuals who will be reading your research paper. You should ask yourself the following: "Is this a topic I might write a master's thesis or a doctoral dissertation on in the future?" If your answer is "yes," then this is probably a good topic to begin researching now and building upon in the future. If you are not stimulated and enthused about your research topic, you can hardly expect your readers to be.

We have found that certain themes recur in our written work over the years. These themes make more clear the progress and development of our thoughts and theorizing. For instance, two of us have published a book on poverty issues, and if you examine our writings through the years you can find the germ of ideas that are expressed in that book. Similarly, the other author of this text has written extensively about library research, and her previous work certainly provided a great deal of background for this book. Often students believe that it is cheating to use the same topic for papers they write at different points in their educational careers. We believe strongly that if students are always elaborating their thoughts and doing new research on the topic to keep current in the field, then they are not plagiarizing from themselves. The most interesting master's theses and doctoral dissertations are those that show that the writer's thoughts have evolved over a period of time, most often several years.

One important thing to remember in writing a research paper or a review of the current literature on a topic is that your personal experiences may have some tangential relevance to the topic, but they may or may not be appropriate for inclusion in the final paper itself. For instance, if you are writing about physical violence in dating relationships and you have experienced this firsthand, you might insert a note to this effect in the foreword or introduction merely to explain to the reader what has prompted your interest in this subject. Or, you might use your case as an example of a certain theory after you have reviewed and written about the existing literature on this theory. It is also likely that personal experience will not be included in the paper at all. Remember that your personal experience represents only a single case study. It may be representative of what many people in relationships have been through, but it may also be a unique pattern of events that only you have experienced. To base an entire paper on a single case study that may or may not be representative of anyone else is a nonscholarly and circular pursuit. No single case study can be considered definitive. As a research paper, the examination of one single case study would yield a very poor grade indeed.

If you choose a topic of interest to you (e.g., physical violence in dating relationships), you must now modify and refine this general topic into an appropriate and workable research question. The title of your research paper should not be a categorical statement. Rather, it is a more scholarly and better form to pose a *research question*. Thus, rather than titling a research paper "The Hell Experienced by Physically Abused Women" (which not only is a categorical statement that their lives are indeed hell but also is very general and vague), you might title your research "Is Violence in Dating Relationships Conceptually Distinct From Violence in Marital Relationships?" Notice that this not only is an open question but also is focused on one specific aspect of understanding the violence in intimate relationships. This is much more feasible to research and write about than the lives of abused women, which would necessarily involve examination of economic, social, occupational, personality, and many other far-ranging issues. You are embarking on a specific research question you are endeavoring to answer or to at least shed some light on. Thus, when you pose the question, it should be balanced and neutral. You truly cannot know what the prior research will indicate until you have thoroughly reviewed it. Try always to formulate a research question rather than posing a categorical statement as the title of your paper. We suggest examining the titles of professional scholarly journal articles to get an idea of what kinds of research questions are posed. In this way you can get some pointers on succinctly and clearly phrasing your research question.

THE BREADTH AND DEPTH OF YOUR RESEARCH QUESTION

Your research question should be sufficiently focused so that you can effectively review the published research and treat your subject within the confines of a 10- or 15-page paper. Your question should not be so microscopically defined, however, that the answers to this question could not possibly be of real interest to people in the field. For example, the research question "Are abused women more likely to push others in supermarket lines?" is most probably neither researchable nor of any real interest to even those people having a basic interest in these individuals.

You will most probably not be able to exhaustively treat whichever topic you choose, but you should pose a research question for which you can locate and review at least five published articles as well as other sources such as books. Remember that you may not find a single article exactly treating your topic of interest. You may have to extrapolate from several articles—to combine findings from different studies and authors and examine the interrelationships among them—to more clearly treat your research question. Thus, you may not find a specific article on the patterns abused women experience in relationships, but in several of the studies you read on this population you might discover tangential findings or statements about their patterns of behavior, even if these articles were not primarily on this topic. One word of caution is in order here: Don't overextrapolate—do not try to write an entire paper based on a few findings that are not strongly related to your topic. Paul Meehl (1960) is a theorist who said that when extrapolating in this way, theorists must "trap" their concept of interest in a "nomothetic net." (Psychologists specifically were of primary interest to Meehl, but these concepts apply equally well, it would seem, to other social science research endeavors.) In other words, one must be able to make sense of the relationships between the different pieces of data and explain why one feels justified in combining them and making some "leaps of logic" in subsequent conclusions.

WHICH VIEWPOINT OR DISCIPLINE WILL YOU FOCUS ON?

You must decide on which viewpoint your research question will be examined from. Will your question be mainly asked from a sociological, psychological, economic, anthropological, political, biological, or historical viewpoint? From the vantage point of which discipline will you ask your research question and focus the research? For example, a research question exploring urban decay and community-building responses to it could be focused each of the following ways (as well as many others, of course):

- Sociological emphasis—Are there more people living below the poverty line in urban America?
- Psychological emphasis—Do youth growing up in decayed urban centers experience negative long-term emotional effects or do they exhibit "resilience"?
- Economic emphasis—What has happened to the tax base in America's urban centers?
- Anthropological emphasis—How do America's urban centers compare to those of Europe?
- Political emphasis—Is there a lower rate of voter registration in America's urban centers?
- Biological emphasis—Is there a higher incidence of lead poisoning in urban centers leading to lower IQ scores by school children?
- Historical emphasis—White flight to the suburbs: to what extent did it really occur?

As one can see, there are many different viewpoints from which to examine an issue. As a student of the social sciences, you should approach the topic from the vantage point of a specific social science; that is, anthropology and cross-cultural studies, sociology, social psychology, psychology, history, economics, criminology, or geography. You might also try to understand your topic from a specific occupational focus, such as criminal justice, human services, or government, that might incorporate any of the social science perspectives. Be as focused as possible while realizing there is often significant overlap between the disciplines.

One word of caution is in order here, especially for social work and psychology students: The fields of social work and psychology in particular frequently adopt the "medical model," and this may not be ideal for your research endeavor. What we mean by the medical model is adopting wholesale and with few modifications the terminology, techniques, and theories from one field and using them in another field for which they may be much less appropriate and applicable.

The field of social work, especially, has relied on information used in the medical field. This is only natural if we look at the history of social work in the United States. (For instance, Mary Richmond, widely considered the "mother of social work," studied with Sigmund Freud, the "father" of psychoanalysis and a medical doctor [a neurologist] himself.) Be careful of placing too much emphasis in your research on the medical model. For example, we have read many papers from undergraduate students examining the questions of possible biological predispositions toward alcoholism.

This can be a trap of sorts for an undergraduate social work or human services student. In a nutshell, the biological research that has been done on this question has failed to explicate a particular gene or chromosome that carries the trait of alcoholism. The field is intensely focused on this question because finding such a gene or chromosome might result in some easy solution to this serious national problem. For a student studying to become a social services counselor, it would be far more interesting and useful in professional development to examine the often neglected psychological and sociological features rather than the biological causes and effects of alcoholism. The important point is to always ask yourself if the vantage point from which you are approaching the research question is the most appropriate and effective one. This will not only result in a more sensible research question, but it will also facilitate your literature search.

Upon reading this chapter, go to the end of this text and locate Worksheet 1: Selecting a Topic and Worksheet 2: Narrowing and Focusing Your Topic. Complete both worksheets and hand them in to your professor.

2

Designing a Search for Scholarly Literature

Once you have selected a topic to research, the next step is to locate information. You will need to search both traditional sources of information in print form, such as books, as well as information found in electronic databases and on the Internet. The best and most effective method of locating the information you need is spending some time designing a search prior to actually searching for the information. Just like making a shopping list before you go shopping is effective, creating a research strategy enables you to make the most of your time when searching for the information and helps you to clearly select the information that meets your research needs. This chapter provides the steps for designing a research strategy to locate information, including choosing correct keywords and selecting the most useful resources to search. The mechanics of the search itself are covered in Chapter 3. You are provided with a worksheet at the end of this text to help you design your own research strategy for your topic.

RESEARCH STRATEGY

1. Step 1 in any search is to develop a question to research. Your question should be interesting, well defined, and narrowly delineated. Refer to Chapter 1 for steps on creating a research question. An example of a research question is:
   Is violence in dating relationships conceptually distinct from violence in marital relationships?

2. Step 2 is to identify the main key words in your research question. Here are the key words from the previous example:

   violence dating relationships marital relationships

3. Step 3 is to develop a list of synonyms for each of the key words you identify. Using a thesaurus to identify possible key words is recommended. You will use these key words to search for information found in electronic format. Using the key words from the example, here is a list of synonyms:

violence in relationships	abuse
dating	physical abuse
marriage	abused women
women or woman	emotional abuse

4. Step 4 is to jot down the names of any scholars and experts on the topic that you are researching. You may access information not only by key words but also by names. For example, Richard J. Gelles has written extensively on the topic of violence in the family. You could input Gelles's name into an online catalog and retrieve his books or search under his name in a database to locate his articles.

5. Step 5 is to refine your topic further by indicating the time period that your research will cover. Will your paper cover research completed in the last 5 years? Will you focus on the past 2 decades? Nineteenth century? Twentieth century? Will you conduct a historical overview of the topic? Or will you do a comparative analysis of 2 or more decades? In our example, we could limit our search to information published from 1990 to the present. However, we might want to look for any major studies that have been done on this topic prior to 1990. Major studies, or what are known as *landmark studies,* provide important background information on a topic. Reading landmark studies on a topic also helps us to place our research question in a contemporary context.

6. Step 6 is to consider from what aspect or viewpoint you will approach your topic. Chapter 1 provides some insights into this. You could research your topic from the economic, legal, psychological, historical, anthropological, or sociologic perspectives. This example, "Is violence in dating relationships conceptually distinct from violence in marital relationships?," could be researched from several perspectives (sociological, psychological, anthropological, etc.) depending upon your own interest.

SELECTING THE MOST USEFUL RESOURCES

We live in a society that is experiencing information overload. Information is available to us in various formats—from print to television to videotape to DVD to the Internet and so on. Your task in any search is to locate the most relevant, current (unless you are taking a historical approach), and credible sources of information. There are significant differences between information that has been peer reviewed in the publishing process and information that has not been read by experts prior to publication.

SCHOLARLY AND POPULAR LITERATURE: MAKING THE COMPARISON

Understanding the differences between scholarly articles and articles published in popular magazines may be a new concept to you. Whether you are giving a presentation or writing a research paper, it is preferable that you cite scholarly sources rather than information found in magazines written for a general audience. These magazines primarily serve the purpose of entertaining their audience, and the information presented may be oversimplified or outdated. Table 2.1 is a brief guide comparing the differences between scholarly journals and popular magazines.

Taking this comparative analysis of information one step further, it is important that you are able to identify different kinds of information in

Table 2.1. A Comparison of Scholarly Journals and Popular Magazines

Scholarly Journals	*Popular Magazines*
Bibliographies or references are included.	Bibliographies or references are usually not included.
Authors are experts.	Authors are often generalists.
Articles are signed by the author.	Articles are sometimes unsigned.
The audience is the scholarly reader, such as professors, researchers, and students.	The audience is the general population.
Standardized formats are followed, such as APA.	Various formats, which are often present.
Articles are written in the jargon of the field.	Articles are written for anyone to understand.
Illustrations, such as maps, tables, and photographs, solely to support the text.	Publications are often profusely illustrated for marketing appeal.
There are few ads.	There are many advertisements.

Note. This table was modified from a handout created by the University of Michigan and from a figure published in "Cooperative Learning in Bibliographic Instruction," by K. N Crook, L. R. Kunkel, and S. M. Weaver, 1995, *Research Strategies* (Winter), pp. 17–25.

order to assess their credibility. One of the easiest ways to identify different kinds of information is to learn the lifecycle of information or, as we refer to it here, the *information chain*. The chain of information, from idea to publication in reference books, is explained in its simplest form. Understand that there are many nuances (political and technical) that occur when information is disseminated to the public. Here, we explain the information chain in the scholarly sense.

For most researchers, the information chain begins with an idea—a curiosity of asking why something is the way it is. A researcher may discuss an idea or question with other experts. Discussion can take place face to face at conferences, via phone or teleconference, or via e-mail. Once a researcher narrows down his or her topic to a specific research question or research statement, a review of the literature is conducted. The literature is reviewed to see if someone else has already studied and answered the research question at hand. If the specific question or statement has not been studied before or needs further research, the researcher designs and conducts a study. This can be a lengthy process involving many false starts and complications. It is not unusual for studies to be piloted, refined, and replicated to make sure results are accurate.

After this study is completed, the researcher writes an article for publication in a scholarly journal. This is how research results get disseminated. To become published in a scholarly journal is no easy task. In writing up the research results, the researcher must determine what journal is most appropriate to publish his or her article and obtain the journal's guidelines for publication. Each scholarly journal, such as the *Journal of Social Psychology*, has specific guidelines that potential authors must follow when submitting an article for publication. These guidelines include such items as margin width, spacing, fonts, style (e.g., APA), and so on. Upon submission of an article, most journals will send one copy of each article to experts in the subject field for review. Each journal has an editorial board of experts who blindly reads the article, meaning that the author's name does not appear on the submitted article. In this manner, the experts can review the article without bias. The experts, who intimately understand the literature in a specific field of study, review the article for content. The journal editor gathers the board's comments and returns the article to the researcher with one of the following three statements:

1. We accept your article for publication.
2. We accept your article for publication if the following changes are made.
3. We reject your article for publication on the basis of . . .

Usually an article will be published in the journal within 18 months of acceptance. Research that is written by the original researcher is considered primary information. The life cycle continues as other researchers read journal articles and write books citing research that has been published in journal form. Information cited by others is considered *secondary* information, or information once removed from the original source. The original research may eventually be cited in an encyclopedia article on the topic. Generally speaking, articles in encyclopedias are considered *tertiary* information, meaning that it is three times removed from the original writers of the research. However, sometimes authors of encyclopedia articles will cite original sources of information, too. If the research is considered "hot" and newsworthy, it does make it to the popular press and media, albeit in a very condensed form. Popular magazines, such as *Time* and *Newsweek* in the United States, may publish a brief column on the topic. Television news shows, such as *ABC News*, *Nightline*, or *CNN's Headline News*, may also mention the story in a short news clip. Periodically, scholarly findings are disseminated in the *New York Times*, often concurrent with their publication in the scholarly journals. While it can take a year or more to clear the scholarly peer review process, a "rough and ready" misinterpretation of the findings may appear suddenly in articles in the popular entertainment media. These articles may pique your interest; however, as a beginning researcher yourself, it is important to locate and read the original research article to fully understand the purpose and conclusions of the original research.

Most, if not all, research in scholarly publications goes through this chain-of-information process to become published. The rigors of this publication process ensure that credible research gets disseminated. With the proliferation of information via the Internet, where anyone can publish anything, you must use a critical eye and read information from the Internet carefully. Some Internet sites are now peer reviewed, mirroring the traditional scholarly publication process and requiring the information to go through the same rigorous test as information published in print journals. However, at this time, such sites are few and far between. The best advice we can give you is to read the information you retrieve from the Internet carefully and analyze such information for credibility by looking for bibliographies at the end of the articles and checking the credentials of the authors.

Take a moment after reading this chapter to complete Worksheet 3: Scholarly vs. Popular Literature, Worksheet 4: Best Places for Information, and Worksheet 5: Your Research Strategy, all of which appear in Appendix C.

3

Conducting a Search for Scholarly Literature

Once you have selected a topic to research, created your research strategy, and determined the best places to look for information, the next step is to learn the mechanics of conducting the actual search for the scholarly literature itself. This chapter provides you with some of the more effective ways to access the information you need. Much of the scholarly literature now published is available online, although not all the information you need is available electronically. In some subject areas, such as the social sciences, information you need to read to be informed of your topic is still published in print form. As such, it is useful to understand how information is organized in most academic libraries and how to locate that information effectively and efficiently.

SEARCHING IN THE INFORMATION AGE

How people access information has changed dramatically since this text was first published in 2000. At that time, we presented details on how libraries organize information and how a researcher could retrieve that information easily. Libraries, as physical places, are still very important in today's age of information. New and renovated libraries frequently include cafes, computers, and wireless Internet access. In addition, there has been a dramatic shift of moving information formerly printed in books and paper journals to born digital or reborn digital books and periodicals. The phrase *born digital* means that the information—whether a book or journal article—was first created electronically and may or may not be followed up with a published print version. *Reborn digital* means that the information was originally produced in print or in some other nonprint form, such as on microfilm or microfiche. In these instances, the print and nonprint information is converted to electronic form, usually by scanning the information into a computer software program. As a result, where the information is stored and how you access that information has changed radically. Therefore, this entire chapter has been revised to present current information-seeking strategies. When used, these strategies will assist you with honing-in on and successfully locating the quality information you need.

SEARCHING WISELY

With all the hype about the Internet, people have the misperception that they can obtain all information needed for a research paper by doing a Google or Yahoo! search. At this point in time, this is a myth. Much of what is placed on the Internet is done solely as a commercial or entertainment venture. Peer-reviewed journals—journals that contain research-based material—are still primarily accessible through subscription-based databases and not by doing a search on such favorite search engines as Google or Yahoo!

Scope of the Source

Good researchers conduct literature searches using a combination of online searching through a library's portal, Internet searches, and traditional library research (i.e., using reference books and reading print materials). Before you begin your search, it is suggested that you determine the scope of the source that you are searching. In other words, what kind of information will you retrieve from your search? Here are some questions to guide you in selecting sources in either electronic or print form:

- What am I searching?
  - A Web site?
  - A library online catalog?
  - A database?
- What kind of information is included?
  - Books?
  - Media (e.g., streaming video, MP3 files, podcasts)?
  - Journals?
  - Magazines?
  - Newspapers?
- What time period does the source cover?
  - How many years does it include?
- How current is the information being searched?
  - How often is it updated?

- When it is updated?
- What information is updated?
- Is the information full text (entire documents)?
  - Or citations and abstracts?
  - Or citations only?
  - Or text with images (e.g., pictures, graphs)

Web Portals

The print information available in each library and via online databases varies from university to university. Each library subscribes to different sets of online databases, e-books, and e-journals. Almost all libraries will give you access to their collection of books and media through an online catalog. Depending upon the subject you are researching and the type of information you are searching for, you may need to search a card catalog (think of this as an online catalog in print) or another finding aid. For example, pretend you are researching the topic of communication between women in the 18th century and you need to find evidence of how they communicated with each other. You may discover that obtaining access to correspondence between women in the 18th century requires you to locate the original letters in a library's special collection. Older, yet just as or more important, material is frequently only available by visiting a specific library that holds the information you need. Old letters are a good example of important information that is valuable to the researcher but is not available electronically.

To provide you with easy ways of searching and accessing information in both print and electronic form, almost all college and university libraries now have Web portals. A Web portal is one Web source that is your entrée to the information that the library either has in its collection or makes available to you electronically. Typically, a library's Web portal will give you access to and information about the library's collections, allow you to search the online catalog and access online databases that the library subscribes to, and access quality information in electronic format. You will also find information about the library (e.g., the library's hours, directions to the library), current news about the library (e.g., upcoming events, online newsletters, new databases), and links to related sources of information on campus, such as upcoming lectures, wireless hotspots, and so on. In many cases you can now ask a librarian for assistance online from the library's Web portal. Usually, clicking on an icon that says something like "Ask a Librarian" or "Chat With a Librarian" enables you to have an online conversation with a librarian about what type of information you are looking for and the best places to locate the information. No matter if you are located within the library or outside the library's walls, you can access a library's Web portal as long as you have a computer with Internet access.

Online Catalogs

Most libraries have an online catalog that allows you access to their collections. You can either access the online catalog directly if you have the catalog's Internet address or URL, or you can access the online catalog through the library's Web portal. The catalog may be a link from the Web portal, or the search engine for the catalog may be posted directly on the Web portal's front page. Sometimes library catalogs will have a name, such as Melvyl: The Catalog of the University of California Libraries (http://melvyl.cdlib.org) or BISON: The University at Buffalo Libraries (http://ublib.buffalo.edu/libraries/e-resources/bison). Online catalogs have evolved tremendously in the past several years. Where once you searched a library's online catalog to locate books, music recordings, videos, and journal titles to see if the library had the information you needed in print form, on microfilm or microfiche, or on some other type of media, today the catalog can be your key not only to locating materials owned by the library but also to information available in electronic format. For example, you may be able to search your library's online catalog for books by Sigmund Freud. Once you locate the information about the book, there may be a "hot link" you can click that will take you to a Web site about Freud. Some library's online catalogs will also link you to the electronic format of a journal where, again, a hot link will be provided to retrieve the full text of the articles within a specific journal issue.

You can search a library's catalog by author's name, title, subject, and keywords. Many library catalogs also enable you to refine your search further by date of publication, type of material (e.g., video, CD), call number, and so on. The best approach to starting a search for books on your topic is to visit your library or go to the library's Web site. Searching online catalogs is very easy; instructions are self-explanatory. Note, however, that libraries differ in terms of their physical collections, the databases that each library subscribes to, as well as what information is accessible through each library's online catalog. If all of this seems a bit confusing or you feel overwhelmed by the choices you have to search for information, do not hesitate to ask a librarian for help.

Upon reading this section, locate Worksheet 6: Locating Books, which appears in Appendix C. Complete this worksheet and turn it in to your professor.

INFORMATION ORGANIZED: LIBRARY OF CONGRESS CLASSIFICATION

Another excellent place to begin searching for information on your topic is to browse through your college or university library's book collection. An initial browsing of your library's bookshelves may reveal much relevant information for your research project.

Materials in libraries have been selected by librarians and professors who are experts or have a strong interest in specific topics. In other words, books in a library's collection are selected to meet your learning needs. Chances are you will locate a book or two that contains a chapter on your research topic just by browsing the collection. Browsing a collection can go rather quickly if you are familiar with how books are organized. Almost all college and university libraries shelve their book collections according to the Library of Congress Classification system (LC). In contrast, most school and public libraries use the Dewey Decimal Classification system (DDC). The aim of both is the same: to arrange bookshelves according to the topics covered in the books. Our focus here is on the LC Classification system. One can go from college library to college library, find one particular section such as the "BF" section, and locate books on psychology. LC Classification organizes books by subject. Similar subjects are shelved together, making browsing an attractive option.

Table 3.1 shows the general outline of the LC Classification scheme. It is a good idea to be familiar with the LC Classification schedule, as often sociological topics are cross-disciplinary. This means that books and materials on your topic may not only be found in the "H" section of the library

Table 3.1. LC Classification Outline

A	General Works
B–BJ	Philosophy, Psychology
BL–BX	Religion
C–D	History
E–F	American History
G	Geography, Anthropology, Sports
H–HJ	Social Sciences: Economics
HM–HX	Social Sciences: Sociology
J	Political Science
K	Law
L	Education
M	Music
N	Fine Arts
P–PZ	Language and Literature
Q	Science
R	Medicine
S	Agriculture
T	Technology
U	Military Science
V	Naval Science
Z	Bibliography, Library Science

Table 3.2. LC Classification Section for the Social Sciences

HM	Sociology
HM 251–291	Social Psychology
HN	Social History, Social Problems, Social Reform
HQ	Family, Marriage, Women
HQ 503–1064	Adultery, The Aged, Child Study, Divorce
HQ 1101–2030	Women, Feminism
HS	Societies (Religious, Ethnic, Political)
HT	Communities, Classes, Races
HT 101–384	Urban Sociology, Cities and Towns
HT 601–1445	Social Classes
HT 1501–1595	Races
HV	Social Pathology, Social and Public Welfare, Criminology
HV 5001–5729	Alcoholism
HV 5725–5770	Tobacco Habit
HV 5800–5840	Drug Habits, Drug Abuse
HV 6001–9920	Criminology
HV 6251–7220	Crimes and Offenses
HV 7231–9920	Police, Prisons, Punishment, Reform, Juvenile Delinquency
HX	Socialism, Communism, Anarchism

(sociology) but in other sections as well. For example, if your topic is "Do men who abuse women have a much stronger genetic predisposition toward alcoholism than do men who do not physically abuse women?," you may explore materials found in the "H" section (see Table 3.2) but also in the "R" section (medicine) and "B" section (psychology).

FINDING THE BOOK ON THE SHELF

The letter(s) along with numbers will appear on the spine (side) of the book as a call number. Each book in the library has a unique call number. You can think of a call number as the "address" to a book. Call numbers can be written in two ways:

HV 554 .G3 2004	This form is found in most online library catalogs.
HV 554 .G3 2004	This form is found as a call number on the spine (side) of the book.

Locating a book on the shelf is easy if you take the process one step at a time. Start with the first letter or letters in the call number:

H HF HV HX

Next, look at the second line of numbers:

HV	HV	HV	HV
5	50	554	570

Then, look at the third line of a letter and number(s):

HV	HV	HV	HV
5	50	554	570
.A4	.K12	.G3	.Z20

Finally, look at the last line, which gives a year:

HV	HV	HV	HV
5	50	554	570
.A4	.K12	.G3	.Z20
1997	1993	2007	1980

REFERENCE BOOKS: PRINT AND ELECTRONIC

Basically, a collection of reference books contains materials that you "refer" to and use in a library. Reference books can be encyclopedias, dictionaries, handbooks, statistical sources, atlases, directories, and so on. The reference collection is a great way to read a summary of major landmark studies that have been done on your topic and to obtain statistics to help you understand your research question. Most libraries will have a separate section where they shelve reference books. Some libraries have purchased reference books on CD-ROM or DVD. Increasingly, you will find reference books on the Internet. Reference books on the Internet can be accessed for free or through your library's Web site with an ID and password. Frequently, libraries will purchase reference books, as well as other books, in electronic format. Known as e-books, these reference titles can be accessed by searching your library's online catalog and borrowing the title electronically for a certain period of time—not unlike checking out a regular book. In some cases you can purchase your own personal subscription to a reference book or collection of reference books. No matter what format the reference book is in, you need to read this information with a critical eye for accuracy and reliability. More information about how to evaluate the information you find for quality can be found at the end of this chapter. Following are some of the more useful reference books in the social sciences. Books that are available in both print and electronic form are so noted after each citation.

Borgatta, E. F., & Montgomery, R. J. (Eds.). (2000). *Encyclopedia of sociology*. New York: Macmillan. (Available online through a subscription.)

Diagnostic and statistical manual of mental disorders: DSM-IV-TR (Text Revision) (4th ed.). (2000). Washington, DC: American Psychiatric Association. (Available online through a subscription.)

The encyclopedia of social psychology. (1996). Oxford: Basil Blackwell. (Now available online through a subscription.)

Kuper, A., & Kuper, J. (Eds.). (2005). *The social science encyclopedia*. New York: Routledge. (Available for purchase as an e-book.)

Maddox, G. L. (Ed.). (2001). *Encyclopedia of aging*. New York: Springer.

Physicians' desk reference: Guide to drug interactions, side effects, indications. (1992–1996). Montvale, NJ: Medical Economics Data. (Available online through a subscription.)

Piotrowski, N. A. (Ed.). (2003). *Magill's encyclopedia of social science: Psychology*. Hackensack, NJ: Salem Press.

Ponzetti, J. (Ed.). (2003). *International encyclopedia of marriage and the family*. New York: Macmillan Reference USA.

Publication manual of the American Psychological Association (5th ed.). (2002). Washington, DC: American Psychological Association. (APA-Style Helper 5.1 companion software is available for purchase.)

Stearns, P. N. (Ed.). (1994). *Encyclopedia of social history*. New York: Garland Press. (Available online through a subscription.)

This is not a comprehensive list. New books arrive at the library daily, and libraries add new online databases frequently. This list will get you started locating background information on your topic and help you with reference style. Reference books are usually located in a separate section of the library or online. Ask a librarian for assistance in locating the reference collection in both print and electronic formats.

COMPUTER SEARCH COMMANDS

Unfortunately, presently there is no standardization in the commands you enter into a computer to conduct your search. The following are some useful guidelines for you to remember.

Boolean Search Operators

A Boolean operator is a word that connects keywords in a way the database recognizes. The most common Boolean search operators are AND, OR, and NOT. You can use these words in various combinations to refine your computer database search. Following our research question of "Is violence in dating relationships conceptually distinct from violence in marital relationships?," some examples are:

dating OR marriage — retrieves information about dating or marriage. This is a very broad search.

dating AND marriage — retrieves information about dating and about marriage. Both the words *dating* and *marriage* need to appear in your search. This is a much more refined search than using the Boolean operator OR.

dating NOT marriage — retrieves information about dating but not about marriage. The NOT operator excludes the words that follow it.

Note that some Web sites and databases apply default Boolean operators to a search string. For example, typing in *dating marriage* may return results for either dating OR marriage or dating AND marriage. It is a good idea to read the Web site or database help screens to determine if the system you are searching uses default Boolean operators.

Case Sensitivity

Some computer databases are what is called case sensitive. When you type in your search, be aware that the computer may only accept your search in all lowercase letters or in all UPPERCASE LETTERS. There are databases that allow you to type in your search eItHeR WaY. These are called case-insensitive databases.

Limiting

Computer database programs will sometimes allow you to limit your search in various ways. These include limiting your search by year or years, language, document type (journal, report, etc.), author, journal title, date, and so on. Check the computer help screens to see which limiting capabilities are available.

Truncation

Truncation means that you can type in the root of a word and place a truncation symbol at the end of the word, and the computer will retrieve variations of that word. For example, typing in *rela** will retrieve *relation, relationships, related,* and any other words beginning with *rela*. Symbols used for truncation are not standard across different databases. More common symbols that you will see for truncation are:

rela* (asterisk)
rela? (question mark)

rela# (pound sign)
rela: (colon)

Reading Help Screens

In reality, no one likes to take time to read the help screens when they are searching a database for information. However, good help screens can provide you with tips for conducting an effective search, especially when your search is not resulting in the information you seek. Help screens should give you several important pieces of information, including whether the database is case sensitive or insensitive, the truncation symbol to use, Boolean operators to use, and sample searches you can use to model your own search. Until standardization occurs in searching databases, it is a good idea to read the help screens prior to conducting your search.

Searching Databases for Scholarly Journal Articles

There are many databases you can select to locate scholarly journal articles on your research topic. Because there are so many choices, you may want to ask your professor or a librarian to suggest the best database(s) to search. Another option is to go to your library's Web site and see if a librarian has categorized the databases available to you by subject. For example, using our research topic of abused women, if we were interested in exploring this subject from a sociological point of view, we may elect to search the Wilson Web. If we were interested in exploring this subject from a psychological point of view, we might want to search JSTOR. (Wilson Web and JSTOR are explained more fully in later sections.) Remember that each library may subscribe to databases that another library may not. Frequently, the databases available through your college or university library are selected by librarians and professors in key subject areas studied by you, the student, as well as by researchers connected to the campus. You should be confident that you will find at least one database to search through your library's Web site. If you do not, ask a librarian for assistance.

Searching a database for journal articles is much the same as using a search engine (e.g., Google) for information on the Internet. You select a database to search through your library's Web site by clicking on the name of the database itself. At this point, you may be asked to input an identification (ID) number and password. Why? Libraries subscribe to databases that contain scholarly journal articles—meaning that the library at your campus paid money to a database company so that you, the student, and faculty can access this information. Librarians need a way to control who has access to databases in order to meet the requirements of licensing agreements they sign with database companies. An easy way of doing this is to have each person input their own unique ID number and password. By inputting an ID and password, you will be authenticated, or allowed to access the database. If you do not have an ID and password, ask a librarian or your computer center for help.

Once you have been allowed to access the database, you will have options of doing a basic search or an advanced search. Most basic searches are those where you input your keywords. For example, if you are searching for information on "Is violence in dating relationships conceptually distinct from violence in marital relationships?," you might enter this basic search: *violence AND dating OR marriage*. If this basic search yields too much information, you can narrow your query by conducting an advanced search. Advanced searching enables you to limit your search by year; use Boolean operators such as AND, OR, and NOT; or restrict your search results to the full text of a journal article, an abstract and citations for the article, or citations alone. Here is what an advanced search may look like, using the previous example: *violence AND dating OR marriage*. You could limit further by a range of years (e.g., 2000–2007) and by type of information (e.g., full-text journal articles). Again, these options vary from database to database, but generally, most databases provide you with these choices.

There are questions you will want to ask yourself when you are searching a database for journal articles:

- What journal titles are included in the database? This varies from database to database depending upon the subject(s) covered as well as licensing agreements between each journal publisher and the company that creates the database itself. Some databases may cover only those journals in a specific subject area, such as psychology. Other databases may be broader in scope, covering several subject areas. You may also find the same journal title accessible via several databases. The best approach is to click on the journal title list that is available in the database. The journal title list is usually on the same page where you input your keywords to conduct a basic search. You can quickly skim the journal title list to see if the database contains the types of journals you are interested in reading.
- What is the coverage, in terms of years, of the database? For example, does the database cover the most recent 5 years of journals? Or does the database go back 10 years or 15 years? More? Sometimes you will have the option of searching a database that contains the more recent articles, as well as searching a second database of the same name but one that contains older articles. A database that contains such articles is sometimes referred to as a retrospective database.
- What is the "lag time" of the database? Most databases have a lag time between the time the journal is published to the time the journal actually

appears in the database. The lag time could be a week, a month, every quarter, or twice a year. This is important if you are searching for a very recent article. For example, you may be searching for an article that appears in the December 2007 issue of *Social Casework*. The database you are searching, say for example, Wilson Web, may only include journals up to November 30, 2007. If this happens, ask the librarian if the library subscribes to the print version of the journal. If it does, you can locate the print version of the December 2007 issue of *Social Casework* and flip through the issue to locate the article you want.

- Is the database full text? Partially full text? Abstract and citation? Or citation only? Most people assume that all databases contain the complete text of each article. This is a misunderstanding. Some databases are full text—meaning that the full text of each journal is included in the database. If this is the case, you only need to search the database for articles on your topic, find your articles, and either print out the articles, download the articles onto a disk or thumbnail USB, or e-mail them to your e-mail address. Some databases are partial full text. This means that you might find the full text of an article you seek, or you will retrieve the complete citation to the article along with an abstract or just the citation to the article. An abstract is usually a 250-word-or-less paragraph that summarizes the key points of the journal article. If you retrieve a citation to an article along with an abstract or just a citation, you can search your library's online public access catalog (OPAC) to see if the library has the journal in another form (e.g., print) or if you can obtain the article through interlibrary loan. Sometimes, databases contain only citations to articles found in journals. This means that you will retrieve the information needed to locate the article in the journal (i.e., author(s) of article, article title, journal title, issue date of journal, volume and issue numbers, and page numbers of journal article). See later sections for more information on how to obtain articles when you only have a citation or citation and abstract to go by.

Here is a brief example of the kind of information you will find when comparing databases. The databases are those available through the American Psychological Association (APA). This type of information will assist you in selecting the databases you wish to search.

- PsycBOOKS is a database of more than 1,400 books and chapters in books from APA. The copyright dates of more than 700 books range from 1950 to 2002. There are 700 archival psychological resources, along with 1,500 entries from the APA/Oxford University Press *Encyclopedia of Psychology*. APA updates PsycBOOKS monthly.

- PsycCRITIQUES contains book reviews in the area of psychology. This searchable database is updated weekly and includes about 15 reviews per week—all from the most recent copyright year. PsycCRITIQUES replaces the print journal *Contemporary Psychology: APA Review of Books*. The final print issue of *Contemporary Psychology* was December 2004.
- PsycEXTRA includes information geared toward professionals in the field of psychology. Quality information gleaned from various sources, such as documents, newsletters, government reports, and so on, are searchable through PsycEXTRA. A source that compliments PsycINFO (a database that provides access to scholarly journals in psychology), PsycEXTRA provides the searcher with abstracts and citations, as well as much full-text information.

A word of caution here: most researchers (students and faculty alike) take the path of least resistance when searching for information. People are more apt to select journal articles or books that are immediately available to them: the book is on the shelf, or the journal is full text on the database. However, you may retrieve an article that is directly on point of your topic, but the database only gives you a citation to the article (not the complete text of the article). The same is true for a book. You may have a citation to a book, but your library does not have the book. Instead of changing your topic to come in line with the books that are readily available in the library or with the full text of journal articles, obtain the articles through your library's interlibrary loan service. (See later in this chapter for more information on interlibrary loan.) If you do this, you will end up with a more satisfying research paper or project rather than writing a paper on a topic that you are not really interested in.

A Word About Wilson Web

As mentioned previously in this chapter, you will have several choices to search for your scholarly journal articles. One of the more common choices is known as the Wilson Web. The Wilson Web is actually a gateway, or portal, to many different types of databases. Not all libraries have access to the Wilson Web, so be sure to check your library's Web site or ask a librarian if you will have access to it.

The main Web page of the Wilson Web provides you with access to such subject-specific databases as Social Sciences Full Text and to databases that cover many subjects, such as the Wilson OmniFile Full Text. The Wilson Web interface allows you to select the databases you want to search and then input your keywords and any other limits you want to place on the search (e.g., limit to year of publication, page image, full text). In clicking on the search icon, you are searching across all the databases you selected to search. Additionally, the H. W. Wilson Company (producers of Wilson Web) has designed their interface to be easily searched by disabled users. If you have access to the Wilson Web, it is a good place to begin your search for scholarly journal articles on your topic.

The H. W. Wilson Company has been around since 1898. They are known for providing quality information. With the overhaul of their Web interface in December 2002, the Wilson Web has come to be known as a solid source of journal articles indexed in a number of databases from a variety of subject disciplines. Its robust search engine enables the searcher to refine a search as needed. Note that almost half of the journal articles you will retrieve via Wilson Web will be full text. The rest of the articles contain a complete citation, many with an abstract. (To obtain articles that only have a citation or citation and abstract, see the section on interlibrary loan.)

A Word About JSTOR

JSTOR initially started as a solution to the shortage of shelf space that many libraries experience. Most academic libraries have back issues of a number of journal titles, some going back a few years, with many going back almost 100 years and more! Created by William G. Bowen, president of the Andrew W. Mellon Foundation, the concept of JSTOR sought to alleviate the shortage of shelf space in libraries while giving libraries another option to preserve their journals and to enhance access to articles found within these journals. As such, those libraries who participate in JSTOR have their journals scanned electronically into a searchable database.

Access to JSTOR is available only if you are a student, faculty, or researcher associated with an institution that participates in JSTOR or via an individual account through any of the participating publishers. Institutions located in the United States as well as others worldwide participate in JSTOR. If your library participates in JSTOR, you will have access to many scholarly journals, such as *American Journal of Sociology* and *American Sociological Review*. JSTOR is best used when you are searching for older journals—those journals that are between 2 and 5 years old. Scanning begins with the first issue of each journal included in the database. Several journals date back to the 1800s!

Depending upon your research topic, you may search more than one database. Searching for information can be considered a controlled trial-and-error process. You begin with identifying possible keywords to locate information on your topic. Using these keywords and their synonyms, you select databases that include journals on your subject area to search. Be open to using different combinations of your keywords and synonyms, limiting your search by year(s), and truncating roots of words. Remember, there is no perfect search! Librarians and researchers find information using the methods explained in this text. Sometimes the first search works; sometimes it doesn't. Keep trying keywords, synonyms, and the last names of experts in the subject field you are researching. In this manner, your search for information is not a wild goose chase nor is it so confined as to not have flexibility. You have established intellectual boundaries within which you can use combinations of words to locate the information you seek.

Obtaining an Article Through Interlibrary Loan

Taking advantage of a library's interlibrary loan service opens up an entire world of information to you. Interlibrary loan is just that—the loaning of materials between libraries for the people who use libraries. Most interlibrary loan services are free. However some libraries may charge a modest fee. You can use interlibrary loan to obtain books or journal articles that are not available in your library. Books can usually be borrowed for several weeks. Journal articles are usually photocopies that are mailed or faxed to the library or are articles that have been scanned into electronic form then e-mailed to you directly. Journal articles do not need to be returned, but you do need to return the books. Note that other media (e.g., videos, films, computer software) are not available through interlibrary loan.

Following is a generic example of searching one database for journal articles on dating and marital violence. For the purposes of this example, consider the database to be one that contains citations to journal articles in the social sciences. Entering the following search into a database will retrieve with the words *women* or *woman* and *dating* or *marriage* or *marital* and *violence* or *violent*.

SUBJECT WORDS:	women or woman
2nd SUBJECT:	dat: or mar:
3rd SUBJECT:	violen:
PERSON'S NAME:	
TITLE WORDS:	
JOURNAL NAME:	
YEAR:	

This search originally yielded 27 citations to scholarly journal articles and book reviews on our topic. Following is one citation from this search.

LIBRARY OWNS. CHECK THE ONLINE CATALOG FOR HOLDINGS.

AUTHOR:	Carlson, Bonnie E.
TITLE:	Dating violence: a research review and comparison with spouse abuse
SOURCE:	Social Casework (ISSN: 0037-7678) v 68 p 16–23 January '87

SUBJECTS COVERED: Women/United States/Crimes against
Dating violence
Wife abuse

Reading this citation is easy and straightforward. The author is Bonnie E. Carlson. The title of the journal article is "Dating Violence: A Research Review and Comparison With Spouse Abuse." This article appears in the journal *Social Casework*, volume 68, in the January 1987 issue, on pages 16–23. The subjects included in this article are crimes against women in the United States, dating violence, and wife abuse. The ISSN is the international standard serial number used by libraries to locate this journal electronically through interlibrary loan. This citation seems very pertinent to our research question, as the article discusses both dating violence and marital violence, so it would be a good article to locate and read.

To locate this journal article in the library, check the library's holdings (or list) for periodicals. Most libraries have a list of all the periodicals (magazines, journals, and newspapers) the library subscribes to. This list may be in paper format or available on the library's online catalog. Remember to check the title of the journal. In the citation above, you would check to see if the library had the journal *Social Casework*. You need volume 68, the January 1987 issue, and you need to read pages 16 through 23. Most libraries will allow you to copy the pages for a nominal fee (if the journal is available in print in the library) or will let you borrow the journal. If the library does not have the journal you need, you have several choices:

- Check other libraries in your geographic area to see if they subscribe to the journal you need. College, university, and large public libraries subscribe to scholarly materials. You may not find scholarly journals in your small local public library. Most libraries have access to journals and books other libraries own (e.g., http://www.wnylibraries.org). Ask a librarian to see if you can access the holdings of other nearby libraries. Once you locate where your journal is, you can drive to that library and find the material.
- Ask a librarian about the library's interlibrary loan service. Interlibrary loan is a free service in most libraries. Through this service, the library will request a copy of your journal article to be sent from another library. Books may also be requested through interlibrary loan. You usually can borrow the book for several weeks and then return it to the library. Media (videos, films, computer software, etc.) are usually not available through interlibrary loan. Allow at least 2 weeks for your materials to arrive from other libraries.
- Another option is via the Internet. There are periodical services available through the Internet where you can electronically order the journal article you need. The service will fax, mail, or electronically send

the article to your home or office. Known as document delivery services, these companies, such as HighBeam Research (http://www.highbeam.com) are fee based, not free.

Remember, this is an example of an initial search for scholarly journal articles from a generic social sciences database. If you do not retrieve the information you are looking for through your first search, you will need to go back and revise your search. Be patient. Part of conducting research to find the right information for your paper is thinking of the appropriate keywords that match the information you are seeking for your research project. This intellectual game takes time.

Once you have completed reading this section, turn to Worksheet 8: Locating Scholarly Articles, which appears in Appendix C. Complete the worksheet and hand it in to your professor.

SEARCHING THE INTERNET EFFECTIVELY FOR INFORMATION

The Internet can be a useful tool for finding information on your topic as long as you look at the information with a critical eye. You need to keep in mind that the Internet is not a replacement for traditional library research, but it is an integral part of your search for information. Libraries continue to house books, magazines, journals, newspapers, and media, such as videos, CDs, and DVDs, that you will use for your research. The Internet, specifically the World Wide Web (or the Web), provides you with information housed on computers and computer servers worldwide. Searching the Web will give you access to personal home pages and institutional, business, and government Web sites as well as information in the public domain. It will also give you access, for a fee, to commercial information, indexing, and databases.

At this time, much of the information found on the Internet is self-published. Almost all information found on the Web is not in any way peer reviewed. In other words, it is not evaluated by an editorial board or a panel of experts as articles in scholarly journals or books are evaluated. Such information is known as *fugitive literature*—information that has not gone through the rigors of analysis by experts in a particular field of study. As a result, you need to critically look at the information you find on the Internet. In Appendix C, Worksheet 9: Evaluating Internet Information can help you evaluate information that is located on the Web.

The Actual Internet Search

You will learn more about how to search the Internet effectively for information in class or from instruction by librarians at, or online through, the library. The following are some key tips to aid your search.

http://Address

The quickest way to search the Internet for information is by http://address. Also known as a Uniform Resource Locator (or Universal Resource Locator), the URL is the fastest way to get to a specific site. Most URLs begin with *http://*. Depending on the version of the browser you are using (Netscape, Internet Explorer, etc.) to search the Internet, you may or may not need to type in *http://* or even the *www* that begins most URLs. An example of a URL is http://www.loc.gov.

Search by Directory

You can also search for information on the Internet by using a directory. A directory is simply a list of broad categories, such as art and humanities, business and economics, education, science, social sciences, and so on. You simply "surf the 'Net" by pointing your computer mouse to a specific category and clicking on it. Many search engines that are available on the Internet also have directories. One of the most useful directories is Yahoo! (http://www.yahoo.com).

Using a Search Engine

You can also search the Internet by typing your topic into a search engine. There are more than 250 search engines to choose from. A few of the more frequently used search engines are:

- Google (http://www.google.com)
- HOTBOT (http://www.hotbot.com)
- Lycos (http://www.lycos.com)
- Yahoo! (http://www.yahoo.com)
- Webcrawler (http://webcrawler.com)

Most search engines have a simple search query and an advanced search query. Some search engines (e.g., Google), have a spell-check feature that suggests alternate spellings when search terms retrieve few items. The advanced search query enables you to use Boolean operators, such as AND, OR, and NOT, to refine your search. You will not find standardization in regard to search engines. If your search is not retrieving the information you need, read the help screens to make sure you are entering your search correctly. Also, try different search engines to retrieve different results. You may also want to search a meta search engine, one that searches across many search engines at once. Meta search engines you might want to try are:

- Dogpile (http://www.dogpile.com)
- Savvy Search (http://search.com)

More information on search engines can be found by going to the SearchEngine Watch Web site at http://searchenginewatch.com as well as University of California, Berkeley, Library's "Finding Information on the Internet: A Tutorial" at http://www.lib.berkeley.edu/TeachingLib/Guides/Internet/MetaSearch.html.

Other Web sites provide you with citations to articles in magazines or journals. There are Web sites that give you the full text (the entire text) of articles, as well as sites that will give you a wide variety of choices through a menu of databases. You can also access information subscribed to by the library from computers outside of the library (also known as accessing information remotely) via the Internet. Almost every library now has a Web site that provides access to a wide range of information. Note that the Web site of each library is unique and that not all libraries give you access to the same information. One library may subscribe to certain databases that you can access remotely and use for your research, while another library will limit access to databases from within the library itself due to licensing restrictions. Another library may not subscribe to the database you need. For the most part, your college or university library Web site will give you access to the scholarly information you need, while your local public library may provide access to information geared to the general public, such as leisure reading or consumer health information rather than scholarly journals.

After you have gained some knowledge about your topic from reference sources, using the college or university library's Web site is a great next step. Librarians create library Web sites (also known as gateways or portals) to assist students and faculty in finding the information they need by selecting quality Web sites and databases on different topics. An example of a portal developed by an academic library is the University at Buffalo Libraries portal that can be located at http://ublib.buffalo.edu/libraries. These sources of information are often organized by subject area and title for easy access through the library's main Web page. The Web page will link to the library's online catalog, along with quality Web pages on different topics as well as databases that the library subscribes to for you to search. (The latter often requires you to input an ID and password before you can search it.)

EVALUATING THE INFORMATION YOU FIND

It is always necessary to evaluate the information you locate, regardless of the format (e.g., print, computer, video) the information comes in. This series of questions will help you identify quality information. Ask yourself the following:

- Is the source considered authoritative? Are the author(s) and the publication considered to be respected, valid sources? What are the author's credentials?
- Is a bibliography or list of references included?
- Is the information applicable for your topic?
- Is this information current, or is it outdated? When was it published?
- Does this source appear to be largely objective and unbiased? Is it opinion or fact based?
- Does the information (facts and data) appear to be accurate? (You may need to compare the facts and data found on the Internet to other sources of information to check for accuracy.)
- Is the information based on primary research, or is it secondary or tertiary information? (That is, is the information based on secondhand or thirdhand information?)
- What is the purpose of the information?
- Who is the audience?

Evaluating information is especially important in the electronic information age. Quality, reliable, and accurate sources of information, such as articles published in peer-reviewed journals and books from reputable publishers, contain certain characteristics. As discussed throughout this book, such items as a bibliography that appears at the end of a journal article or book, indication of an author's credentials, the date the information was published, and whether the piece you are reading is an opinion piece or one based on research, are important characteristics to look for in quality sources. Remember, books and journals are frequently accessible via the Internet as well as published in print.

The challenge with assessing the quality of what you are reading appears when you are reading information via the Internet. Why? Anyone can write anything and claim to be an expert on any topic, particularly on the Internet. Most information contained on Web sites on the Internet are not peer reviewed, meaning that the information has not gone through the rigorous process of review by experts in a specific subject area prior to publication in any format. As such, you need to remain skeptical of such sources. There are several steps that you can take if you are unsure the information you retrieved is credible. Search for the author's name in other sources to see if he or she has written books or journal articles on the topic. Look for the author to be listed in biographical reference books for his or her credentials. Look for the author's name in bibliographies of sources you have retrieved. Searching for an author's credibility can be challenging. Ask a librarian if you need help.

ASKING FOR ASSISTANCE

As stated earlier in this chapter, you may feel a bit overwhelmed by the sources available to you to search for information. There are OPACs where you can find books, videos, and possible journals in electronic format on your topic. There are databases—some free, some available commercially only through your library with an ID and password—where you can locate scholarly journal articles or, at minimum, the citation to a journal article that you may be able to locate at your library or obtain through interlibrary loan. And then there is the Internet, where you will find a lot of information but not necessarily quality information. Here, as with other forms of electronic information, you will need to sift through, read, and cull the best information for your paper or project.

If you need assistance at any time, do not hesitate to ask a librarian for help. Librarians have completed a master's (graduate) degree in the field of library and information science. In graduate school, librarians learn how to look for information and where to locate the best information on a topic. A librarian can be your link between your topic and the information you need. At most libraries, you can contact a librarian in several ways: by walking into the library and asking the librarian for assistance, by phoning the library, or via the Internet through services commonly referred to as "virtual reference service." Some libraries are staffed with librarians who may have a second master's degree in a specific field of study, such as criminal justice or psychology. These librarians are considered subject specialists—meaning they have more depth of knowledge on specific topics. You can usually make an appointment with a librarian, including a subject specialist. This individual consultation can be very useful to you, especially if you have a detailed project to research. If you make an appointment for consultation, make sure that you come prepared with specific questions you need answers to as well as some sense of the type of information you are seeking (e.g., books, videos, journal articles).

Connecting to a virtual reference service is easy. You can connect to an actual librarian by going to your library's Web site and looking for the service. Like OPACs, virtual reference services can be called different names (e.g., AskUs24/7 or Instant Librarian). Most virtual reference services are available 24 hours a day, 7 days a week, so that you need not wait for the library to open to ask a question. To see if your library offers a virtual reference service, go to the library's Web site. Locate the icon to the service (if it's there), click on it, and you will be connected to a librarian who will conduct an online chat with you or will e-mail you with places to look for information. With some virtual reference services, the librarian will be able to "push" Web pages to you and teach you how to search for information through a feature called "cobrowsing." At the end of the chat session, the librarian will e-mail you the transcript of your online session along with links and citations to the information referred to during your session. The point here is not to be shy or not to think that your questions are stupid. Librarians are there to assist you in meeting your information needs. They get all kinds of questions. All you need do is ask, and they will help you.

Take a moment to complete Worksheet 9: Evaluating Internet Information, which appears in Appendix C.

4

Outlining the Research Paper

Before you can really begin outlining your paper, you should have a sense of what information is available. As you look through the literature, you will begin identifying some key points. As your paper cannot possibly be exhaustive—you cannot cover everything—you may have to refocus your research question. You will need to identify areas of information that address your question and limit your paper to a few of these. We refer to these as "key points." For instance, in our example paper (see Appendix B), the research question we pose is: "Is violence in dating relationships conceptually distinct from violence in marital relationships?" This question is asked from a sociological perspective, and we are interested in examining dating violence as a form of intimate violence. There is so much information on dating violence that our focus must necessarily be limited. Bring yourself wholeheartedly into the decision-making process on the direction of your paper, and decide what areas or points of information you will address. Do not expect to cover everything, or you will soon become overwhelmed.

Choose key points that make sense together. You definitely want to review a lot of information about a few points rather than a little information about many points. When you try to cover too many areas, your paper begins to look more like a checklist rather than a well-thought-out research review. Remember: Your professors can tell the difference! Also remember: Your professors have been where you are now!

You will soon find in your literature review that, in order to have a comprehensive response to your question, you need to review and include literature that does not focus on, or possibly does not even address, your specific topic. By the same token, you will find that much of the literature written on your primary topic of interest is not relevant for your paper. If for no other reason than this, plan on reviewing a lot of literature and going into areas related to, but not necessarily focused on, your topic. You will be able to make some interesting connections between various pieces of information that relate directly to your question and add substance to your paper. Once again, you will be using your own critical-thinking skills to bring the various pieces together in a way that makes sense. This is a creative and challenging process. In time, and with practice, we believe you will find the process enjoyable and enlightening. At the very least, it will certainly come to seem less onerous and intimidating.

It should be clear by now that before you can produce an effective outline, you should have a working knowledge of the literature. Once you have this working knowledge and before you go extensively into the next step, which we call "taking notes while reading," you are ready to form an outline. A rough or preliminary outline is essential because it will help you not only in organizing and writing your paper but also in guiding your search for relevant information. To give you an idea of what goes into developing an outline, we present the process that was involved in outlining our example paper, which is found in Appendix B of this manual. You may also follow this procedure for your presentation. (Please refer to Chapter 8 for more details on preparing a presentation.)

THE OUTLINE

Introduction

Always have an introduction to your paper. The introduction must include your specific research question. You should also state the specific key points you will address in the order that you will address them. You might include some fundamental information in the introduction, such as why this is an important area to study—a brief explanation will do—and how many people are affected by your topic. If not in the introduction, you should include somewhere in the paper how many people are affected by your topic—basic statistical information—and do not forget to cite where that information comes from. If different sources provide different statistics, that is perfectly acceptable; simply state the differences. At some point you may want to include an explanation of why different sources provide different figures. This can possibly be an integral part of your paper. (For a final paper example, see Appendix B, Paragraph 1.)

Key Point 1

Begin listing the main parts of key point 1. In the final paper, you will have a review of the literature focused on this first point. (For a final paper example, see Appendix B, Paragraphs 2 through 4.)

Key Point 2

Begin listing the main parts of key point 2. In the final paper, you will have a review of the literature focused on this second point. (For a final paper example, see Appendix B, Paragraphs 5 through 7.)

Key Point 3

Begin listing the main parts of key point 3. In the final paper, you will have a review of the literature focused on this third point. (For a final paper example, see Appendix B, Paragraphs 8 through 14.)

Conclusion

Always have a conclusion. At the very least, this should sum up the paper. You may provide some of your own insights—always based on the literature review. You may make suggestions for further research in this area. (For a final paper example, see Appendix B, Paragraph 15.)

Reference List

The American Psychological Association (APA) refers to the full citations of all sources cited in the text as the reference list. All the sources that are cited in the text must have full citations on the reference list page. If a source has a full citation on the reference list page, it must be cited at least once in the text of your paper. If you are using the APA format for citing sources (explained in Chapter 6), then you should not include any uncited sources on the reference list page.

You may keep a working bibliography, which is a more comprehensive reading list but not the same as the reference list. The outline becomes a working guideline for you. Some sections become longer and more complex than other sections, which is fine. Your paper should have the necessary information to introduce the reader to the problems under consideration. In our case, key point 1 and key point 2 provide a foundation for examining the research question in more depth. Undergoing the process of outlining the paper helps you to organize the literature you have been reviewing. The outline might be considered a work in progress, as you will probably revise it as you go along. Notice the list of authors and the year their works were written. These are the authors and their research that will be included in the paper. The same author may be included in different parts of the paper as the material applies. Remember, unless there is a compelling reason to do otherwise, you should present studies and events in chronological order. Thus, it would be more sensible to present early, "classical" research on your topic followed by more contemporary, recent research than vice versa. If, however, for reasons of individual style or effect you wanted to refer to the most recent study and then work your way backward, there is no firm rule against doing so.

EXAMPLE PROCESS OF DEVELOPING AN OUTLINE

In developing key points to be focused on in your paper, you will probably find that your topic needs to be understood within a larger context. This might be a good place to start. How does your topic fit into a larger field of study? In researching dating violence, it soon becomes clear that this is one area of study within the larger field of family violence.

Example of an Outline

Our outline looks like this:

Introduction
Research Question: Is violence in dating relationships conceptually distinct from violence in marital relationships?
Key point 1: Dating violence may be understood as a form of family violence or, more precisely, intimate violence.
Key point 2: The role of dating and courtship in society must be examined.
Key point 3: Dating violence is understood as being conceptually distinct from violence between spouses and cohabitating partners.

Key point 1: Dating violence may be understood as a form of family violence or, more precisely, intimate violence.

- A. Dating violence research is one area of study within the larger field of family violence.
    1. short history of research of family violence
    2. extent of family violence (Straus & Gelles, 1990; Steinmetz, 1977–1978)
        - a. family violence research laboratory
        - b. violence by men toward women
        - c. violence by parents toward children
        - d. violence by women toward men
    3. theoretical focus of research not limited to male domination and female subordination (Stets & Pirog-Good, 1989; Lobel, 1986)
- B. Violence between intimate others is not limited to married couples.

Key point 2: The role of dating and courtship in society must be examined.

- A. Research on dating violence demonstrates the need to recognize violence that occurs in dating and courtship. (Makepeace, 1981)
- B. There is a romantic love complex. (Clausen, 1986; Lott, 1987)

Key point 3: Dating violence is understood as being conceptually distinct from violence between spouses and cohabitating partners.

A. Research links childhood violence, dating violence, and marital violence. (Makepeace, 1981, 1989; Roscoe & Benaske, 1985; Stets & Straus, 1990)
B. Define the terms *dating, cohabitating,* and *marriage* as used in the research on violence. (Burke, Stets & Pirog-Good, 1988; Carlson, 1987; Makepeace, 1981; Martin, 1976; Dobash & Dobash, 1979; Stets & Straus, 1990; Sugarman & Hotaling, 1989)
C. Explore the structure of the relationship and extent or type of violence used. (Stets & Straus, 1990)

Conclusion
Reference List

In essence, then, our three key points tie together well and seem to adequately address our research question. Our paper focuses on some very basic information in the field of dating violence. It provides a foundation for us to build our understanding of the social context of dating violence. Our focus also provides us with a fundamental understanding of history of the research on dating violence as it developed in the overall field of family violence. Please note that it can be extremely beneficial for you to review the history of research on your particular area of interest in building your expertise in the subject area.

Upon finishing this chapter, locate Worksheet 10: Outlining the Research Paper, and begin filling it in.

5

Taking Notes While Reading

You will be examining a number of sources for your paper. These sources may be primary sources, secondary sources, or tertiary sources. Primary sources are articles, books, or other types of work, such as diaries and manuscripts, that are written by the original researcher on original work. These primary sources are, of course, preferable to secondary or tertiary sources. However, sometimes you cannot locate the primary sources on a particular study or data set. If you have made an earnest attempt to locate the original source but have been unable to, it is acceptable to use a secondary source that alludes to the original research. You must, however, make it clear that you have referenced from a secondary rather than a primary source. Secondary sources refer to the work of others, such as is found in books that provide an overview of literature on a particular topic or in the literature review section of an article. Tertiary sources refer to a source's source—three times removed from the original source. Reference books are considered tertiary sources. For your own research, you may use a tertiary source, such as an encyclopedia, for guidance. You should not, however, rely on that source for your paper. Rely most heavily on primary and secondary sources. Eventually you will find that you want to have a heavy emphasis on primary sources.

WHAT YOU SHOULD LOOK FOR IN JOURNAL ARTICLES

You should include information from scientific journal articles in your research paper. Reading these articles is time consuming and requires a bit of technical skill. Being familiar with the format of the article is very beneficial.

Undergraduate students are often mystified by their first exposure to scholarly, professional journal articles. They may contain jargon, references to statistical analysis procedures that seem incomprehensible, and complex, sophisticated theories that the student has not heard of. Keep in mind the following rule: Do not report on something you do not understand! However, do not put an article aside because you do not want to take the time to comprehend it. Distinguish which articles are too difficult for you to understand versus those that simply require extra time and effort. Put aside the difficult articles and continue.

Scholarly journal articles usually begin with an abstract, which is a very short summary of the article itself. Start by reading this summary. If the article appears to be on your topic and of interest to you, read on.

In reading the article, you should try to break it down into sections. Most likely—unless the article is actually a broad survey of past literature or a literature review article—the article is reporting on primary research; that is, research conducted by the author or authors. This makes the article a primary source, and that is what we are concerned with now. The article may be written by one or more authors.

Journal articles are usually written in a sequence that follows the methods of carrying out a study. This is generally referred to as the scientific method. While this book is not the place to learn all of the possibilities for carrying out a study, we can give you some guidelines for reading the articles that result from such studies. In fact, in order to conduct good research following the steps of the scientific method, the authors must conduct a literature review. In order for students to conduct a literature review using journal articles, you must understand the basics (at least) of the scientific method.

The scientific method can be broken down to specific parts. These are the foundation, the research design and data collection, data analysis, and conclusions. If the article has a section called methodology, this probably incorporates the research design and data collection sections.

The foundation, often called the introduction, really sets the stage for all that is to come in the article. In the foundation, the question is established—what the author wants to know. A review of the literature explains why the problem is an important one to understand, what other people know, and where the gaps are in the research. The authors may introduce a theoretical understanding of the problem in this section. The theoretical piece is the key to how the author or authors approach and conceptualize their research question. If there is a hypothesis, it is usually derived from a combination of the research question, the literature review, and the theory. Very simply, a hypothesis is a statement that is going to be tested using empirical data. Empirical data is information that can be gathered using the methods of science, information that can be observed in some fashion.

There may not be a hypothesis if the research is exploratory in nature. An exploratory study seeks to find out as much as possible about a topic so that more specific questions may be asked. The study may also be descriptive. In this case the study tries to describe the problem as much as possible. Because the goal of science is to explain and predict, the study should contribute to this in some way. Explanation and prediction ultimately involve theory.

The research design or methodology section describes how the researcher is gathering information for a study. It may involve experimentation, survey research, participant observation, historical data, or other types of data collection. The possibilities are numerous. You should be familiar with the research design in each article. Note whether the authors are conducting an experiment or a survey. Is the author a participant observer or collecting historical or archival data or something else? Understanding how data is collected is very important in evaluating the study. The authors should also generally explain what the limitations are in any given analysis. Limitations do not make a study invalid—indeed they are inevitable. However, noting the limitations helps guide the reader to an informed understanding of the generalizability of the study.

The data analysis section will cause students the most amount of grief. This section is often extremely technical, involving statistical analyses. This is known as quantitative analysis—involving numbers. Often the scientific method in the social sciences involves turning social life into something that can be measured numerically. It sounds rather odd, but there is logic to it. We strongly encourage students to eventually take a course in statistics—especially if you plan to continue in the social sciences. Indeed, this may be a requirement!

This data analysis section may also be qualitative. In this case, the analysis is conducted using data that is expressed as words, pictures, or objects. This may be more understandable for many students. This type of analysis is often used by anthropologists and historians. However, you may find it useful in other social sciences disciplines, such as sociology or psychology. It is also likely that any given study will use a combination of quantitative and qualitative data. In any case, there is a series of strict guidelines that are established within the disciplines for determining the most appropriate data collection and analysis procedures for scientific research.

For your purposes in writing a social sciences research paper, your instructors will most likely not expect you to comprehend all the procedures, especially if you have not taken a research methods, statistics, or other type of data collection and analysis course. You can cursorily read or skim through the data analysis section and move on to the next section, usually referred to as the discussion or conclusion section.

The discussion and conclusion sections interpret the data analysis. These sections are very beneficial to you, as they discuss the results of the study as interpreted by the authors. The discussion section will make the most sense if you understand the foundation and the methodology sections. If you wish to enhance your understanding of the methods of science, feel free to refer to a book on research methods in the social sciences. Each discipline focuses on a different aspect of social behavior, therefore each discipline uses methods that are applicable to its field. Keep this in mind when looking for an appropriate research methods book to use as a resource.

USING SCHOLARLY BOOKS

You may want to use scholarly books as secondary sources. If a book is written by a recognized authority or authorities and if there is a reference section or bibliography at the end of the book, then you can be assured that this is a legitimate, scholarly source. While you will most heavily emphasize your primary, professional journal sources, some books can provide a useful overview of a great deal of theorizing and research findings.

Always read the preface and introduction to the book, as they will give you a good framework for mentally organizing the material that follows in the rest of the text. Educators sometimes refer to this as setting up a schema or mental diagram beforehand. Many educators have argued that having a schema will give an overall sense of perspective and will make it much easier to comprehend and retain information.

Even if you are only technically focusing on one chapter in a scholarly book, you may want to leaf through or skim the rest of the book. You may be surprised at the useful and relevant information, data, graphics, and so on that a relatively quick perusal can give you.

TAKING NOTES

In your paper, you will often refer to the work of others. You should include as detailed a discussion as is relevant in your paper. Therefore, you should take notes on each of the articles you read. Some general questions you should try to answer on each article are as follows:

- Who is the author(s)?
- What is the author interested in? What is the research question? The article may not contain a specific research question. If not, try to figure out what it might be.

- Why does the author think this research is important? What gap does it fill?
- Does the author refer to any specific theory that is helping to guide the author's thinking about this question? If yes, what is it?
- Is the author testing a specific hypothesis? If yes, what is it?
- What method is the researcher using to collect data? Participant observation? Survey research? Experimentation? A combination of some or all of these? Be as specific as possible (e.g., the researcher conducted a survey using an open-ended interview schedule).
- What is the sample that the author is gathering data about?
- How is the data analysis conducted? Is it quantitative or qualitative or both? This section will be difficult. Do the best you can.
- What interpretation does the author give regarding the data analysis? What conclusions are drawn? If there is a hypothesis being tested, is it supported? Explain and elaborate.

In addition to answering these questions, be sure you write down all of the reference information: author, year published, title of article, journal name, volume number, and pages. Also, if you found the article online, jot down the Internet address and date you accessed the information. You should record all of the citation information for all types of sources, not only journal articles. In addition, you should write down as much information as possible from each source that is relevant to your paper. If you note a particular quote from a source, write down the page number. Do not wait until you start the process of actually writing your paper to try to remember these things. Refer to Chapter 6 for more information.

It may be quite valuable to buy a packet of 100 to 200 index cards and keep a small file box—an old tissue box will do—to order the cards in. Jot down citation information, important points, pieces of data you might want to report on, and direct quotes that you might want to use in the paper. These cards will be useful later for helping you remember what you have read and for outlining your paper. Taking notes on what you are reading is essential in the writing process. It is truly a time-saving device and will lead to a more organized and better cited paper. There is nothing more time consuming or frustrating than searching through a pile of articles and books for a quote you know is there but you just cannot find it! Unfortunately, when this happens you must abide by this rule: If you cannot cite the source, you cannot use the information.

6

The APA Format: Writing and the Use of an Appropriate Format

We have been accused of being sticklers about students' use (or misuse) of format and style in their papers. We believe, however, that using an accepted, organized standard style or format is imperative in writing a paper that will clearly and effectively make its point. Later on in students' careers, they will also find that using the correct format is a minimum standard for publication purposes.

The two most well-known formats are the Modern Language Association (MLA) used in the humanities disciplines and the American Psychological Association (APA) used in most social sciences disciplines. Another common format used by publishing houses is the *Chicago Manual of Style* (*Chicago*), and there may be additional formats in specific subject areas. Check with your professor or a librarian.

THE APA FORMAT

The APA format is one of the many styles used for citing and referencing sources. APA is a well-recognized method utilized in the social sciences. Unless you are requested to do otherwise, we encourage you to use this method for your own papers. While we are providing an overview of this method, libraries carry official publications that explain this format in great detail, and you may look up information about it on the APA style Web site at http://apastyle.apa.org. The examples used here are from the example paper found in Appendix B of this manual. The location of the example is in parentheses for easy reference.

Reference Citations in Text

Document your paper throughout. Unless referring to a specific quote in the work or a specific section, you will be citing by author and date. For the most part, the author(s) will be either (a) the author(s) of a book, (b) the author(s) of a chapter of a book, (c) the author(s) of a journal article, or (d) the author(s) of an electronic reference.

In referencing books, it is important to distinguish between books with one or multiple authors and books that are edited and have one or multiple authors per chapter. If the book has one or multiple authors, this is who you cite. Thus, if you use information from three chapters of a book that has one or multiple authors, you will be citing one source. If you use information from three chapters of a book with one or multiple chapter authors, you will be citing three sources, and these are then referenced according to chapter author(s) on the reference list page. Examples of citing sources in the text follow.

Citing One Work by One Author

APA format uses the author–date method of citation. Use the last name of the author only (do not include suffixes such as *Jr.*) and the year of the publication. These are inserted in the text at the appropriate point:

Example:
What was once thought of as a rare occurrence between family members (Gelles, 1980) is now recognized as a common, often socially accepted phenomenon in many, if not all, types of intimate relationships. (Appendix B, Paragraph 7)

Example:
James Makepeace (1981) was the first to suggest that social scientists examine courtship violence as a link between violence experienced in childhood and later violence experienced in marriage. (Appendix B, Paragraph 7)

Citing One Work by Two Authors

When a work has two authors, always cite both authors' names every time the reference occurs in the text.

Example:
In 1985, the second national survey of family violence was conducted by the Family Violence Research Laboratory at the University of New Hampshire (Straus & Gelles, 1990). (Appendix B, Paragraph 2)

Example:
Straus and Gelles (1990) found in the 1985 National Family Violence Survey that about 161 couples per 1,000 of couples experienced one or more

physical assaults on a partner during that year, and that 34/1,000 wives were severely assaulted (1.8 million) by their husbands. (Appendix B, Paragraph 3)

Citing One Work by Three to Five Authors

When a work has three, four, or five authors, cite all authors the first time the reference occurs. In all additional citations of these authors, include only the first author followed by *et al.* and the year.

Example:
Current studies of dating violence among high school students, for example, by James, West, Deters, and Armijo (2000) found rates of 19% to 59% had been the victim of physical violence. James et al. (2000) studied psychological and physical abuse in a sample of adolescents. (Appendix B, Paragraph 9)

Citing One Work by Six or More Authors

Cite only the last name of the first author followed by *et al.* every time it is used. An exception to this occurs when the first author appears in more than one source and the years are the same. In this case, cite as many names as necessary until the specific sources can be distinguished from each other, and then use *et al.*

Citing Specific Parts of a Source

To cite a specific part of a source, indicate the page, chapter, figure, table, or equation at the appropriate point in the text. Always give page numbers for quotations. If the source is an electronic reference and there are no original page numbers, use the paragraph number, if available, preceded by the paragraph symbol ¶ or the abbreviation *para.*

Example:
For example, Irene Frieze wrote: "Feminist researchers (a group that I consider myself to be a member of) in those decades did not question their assumption that men were the aggressors and women were the victims of marital violence" (2000, para. 2). (Appendix B, Paragraph 4)

Citing Information From Multiple Sources

Often, researchers state similar findings or make similar arguments. Rather than go through each one individually, you may want to summarize the work of more than one source in the same sentence or the same paragraph.

Example:
This is most clear in efforts to understand violence within gay and lesbian relationships (Letellier, 1994; Lobel, 1986; Renzetti, 1994). (Appendix B, Paragraph 4)

Citing Information From Electronic Sources

Electronic sources are varied. APA has guidelines for citing electronic sources and referencing them on their Web site at http://www.apastyle.org. APA explains that it will try to be responsive to the speed at which the electronic environment and electronic language is moving. For the purposes of this text we provide a couple of examples using electronic sources but strongly encourage you to visit the APA Web site to guide you through specific usages.

Two Scenarios

Citing Specific Parts of a Source. If the source is an electronic reference and there are no original page numbers, use the paragraph number, if available, preceded by the paragraph symbol ¶ or the abbreviation *para.* Use the date of publication as listed on the document.

Example:

For example, Irene Frieze wrote: "Feminist researchers (a group that I consider myself to be a member of) in those decades did not question their assumption that men were the aggressors and women were the victims of marital violence" (2000, para. 2). (Appendix B, Paragraph 4)

Citing a Stand-Alone Document With No Author Identified and No Date. If no author is identified, reference the title of the document, and list the date the document was retrieved by you.

Example:

For instance, the Alabama Coalition Against Domestic Violence (ACADV) "is a nonprofit organization dedicated to working toward a peaceful society where domestic violence no longer exists" (2005, para. 1). (Appendix B, Paragraph 11)

Primary Versus Secondary Sources

A primary source provides the original work of the author or authors. A secondary source refers to the fact that the material provided by one source came from another source. Try to refer mostly to primary sources; however, sometimes it is appropriate to cite secondary sources. If so, state the information you find relevant for your paper and cite the source that you got the information from. Do not get caught up in citing your source's sources.

Example:

Another study carried out by Howard and Wang (2003) used survey data from the 1999 Youth Risk Behavior Survey to identify risk profiles of adolescent girls who were victims of dating violence (cited in Johnson, 2005). (an example of citing a secondary source)

You will reference the secondary source in the reference list. Only reference primary source material if you read it and directly refer to it in your paper. Referencing information is for your academic protection. By accurately citing the information you have read and referred to in your writings, you will be ensured that your professor will understand that you took someone else's information as restated or paraphrased by a secondary author.

The Reference List

The reference list at the end of the paper provides all of the material needed to retrieve each source cited in the text. Remember: If it was not cited in the text, it must not be referenced in the reference list. Similarly, if the work is cited in the text, it must be fully referenced in the reference list. Refer to Appendix B's reference list for a complete example.

The sources should be listed alphabetically by the surname of the first author. When referencing several works by one author, they should be arranged by year of publication with the earliest year first. One-author entries precede multiple-author entries beginning with the same surname. References with the same first author and different second or third authors and so on are arranged alphabetically by the surname of the second or third authors and so on.

Authors may also be an agency, association, or institution, or occasionally there will be no author at all. In the first case, alphabetize by the agency, association, or institution. If there is no author, the title moves to the author position. Only use the word *anonymous* if the source states *anonymous*.

Following are examples from books, chapters in books, journal articles, and electronic sources. For each one, note the hanging indentation following the first line, the use of upper and lowercase letters, periods, commas, colons, spacing, italics, and the symbol & in place of the word *and*.

Referencing books with one or multiple authors requires the following:

- Author(s)—first and middle initials (if available) and full surname
- Year of publication
- Title of book
- City of publication
- Publishing company

Example:

Lobel, K. (Ed.). (1986). *Naming the violence: Speaking out about lesbian battering*. Seattle, WA: The Seal Press.

Author:	K. Lobel
Year of publication	1986
Title of book	Naming the Violence: Speaking Out About Lesbian Battering
City of publication	Seattle, WA
Publishing company	The Seal Press

Referencing chapters in books (the chapters have different authors and the book is edited) requires the following:

- Author(s) of chapter
- Year of publication
- Title of chapter
- Editor(s) of book
- Title of book
- Page numbers of chapter
- City of publication
- Publishing company

Example:
Stets, J. E., & Straus, M. A. (1990). The marriage license as a hitting license: A comparison of assaults in dating, cohabiting, and married couples. In M. A. Straus & R. J. Gelles (Eds.), *Physical violence in American families: Risk factors and adaptations to violence in 8,145 families* (pp. 227–244). New Brunswick, NJ: Transaction Books.

Authors of chapter	J. E. Stets and M. A. Straus
Year of publication	1990
Title of chapter	The Marriage License As a Hitting License: A Comparison of Assaults in Dating, Cohabiting, and Married Couples
Editors of book	M. A. Straus and R. J. Gelles
Title of book	*Physical Violence in American Families: Risk Factors and Adaptations to Violence in 8,145 Families*
Page numbers of chapter	pp. 227–244
City of publication	New Brunswick, NJ
Publishing company	Transaction Books

Referencing journal articles from a paper format requires the following:

- Author(s) of article
- Year of publication (if available, also include month and day)

- Title of article
- Journal name
- Volume number
- Issue number (if there is one)
- Page numbers

Example:
Roscoe, B., & Benaske, N. (1985, July). Courtship violence experienced by abused wives: Similarities in patterns of abuse. *Family Relations*, 34(3), 419–424.

Author(s) of article	B. Roscoe and N. Benaske
Year and month of publication	July 1985
Title of article	Courtship Violence Experienced by Abused Wives: Similarities in Patterns of Abuse
Journal name	*Family Relations*
Volume number	34
Issue number	3
Page numbers	419–424

Referencing journal articles from an electronic format requires the following:

- Author(s) of article
- Year of publication (if available, also include month and day)
- Title of article
- Journal name
- Volume number
- Issue number (if there is one)
- Page numbers (if there are any)
- Date the article was retrieved from the electronic source
- Database or URL the article came from

Example:
Howard, D. E., & Wang, M. Q. (2003). Risk profiles of adolescent girls who were victims of dating violence. *Adolescence*, 38(149). Retrieved December 20, 2004, from Professional Development Collection database.

Authors of article	D. E. Howard and M. Q. Wang
Year of publication	2003
Title of article	Risk Profiles of Adolescent Girls Who Were Victims of Dating Violence
Journal name	*Adolescence*

Volume number	38
Issue number	149
Date the article was retrieved from the electronic source	December 20, 2004
Database the article came from	Professional Development Collection

If the author of a document is not identified, begin the reference with the title of the document. If the document is contained within a large and complex Web site, identify the host organization and the relevant program or department before giving the URL for the document itself. Note that there is no period after a URL at the end of a reference.

Example:
Alabama Coalition Against Domestic Violence. (n.d.). Retrieved December 26, 2004, from http://www.acadv.org/about.html

Example:
Yahoo! Search. (n.d.) *Dating violence*. Retrieved January 4, 2005, from http://search.yahoo.com/search?p=Dating+Violence

You will come across still other sources that are not illustrated here in both paper and electronic formats. For example, paper formats include brochures, newspaper articles, classic works, and personal communications. Electronic formats include e-mail, electronic mailing lists, and other Internet sources. In such instances, consult the latest edition of the *Publication Manual of the American Psychological Association* or the American Psychological Associations style Web site at http://www.apastyle.org.

Please take a moment to complete Worksheet 7: Chapters in Books, which appears in Appendix C.

7

The Writing Process Itself: You Can't Edit a Blank Page

At some point in your research and writing, remember that you can't edit a blank page. What we mean is, *begin*! If you commit something to writing, you then have something to work with. Alternatively, if you obsess for weeks about how and where to begin, you will most likely procrastinate until you no longer have enough time to do a good job on the research paper. We have found that the best technique for writing is constructing an outline and then sitting at the word processor, "filling in" the outline with a running stream of consciousness—your thoughts and findings on each of the outline subtopics. This is analogous to a brainstorming process. Try to write at least one page each day this way. In a few weeks, you will have a mainstay of your paper written. Going back later and editing, correcting, adding, and modifying will be much easier once you have this body of writing to work with.

Remember to clearly distinguish your own theorizing and findings from other sources that you have read. The reader must be able to tell at any particular point whether you are speaking for yourself or for others in the field. You cannot simply mass information together without properly crediting each source and conclusion that you have presented in a research paper. On the undergraduate level, and certainly on the graduate level, such a paper will be returned with a very low grade indeed.

When summarizing others' theories and findings, be sure to identify the main points and condense these without losing their meaning. To whatever degree possible, paraphrase. Use your own words to describe what the original author was trying to say. If there is a phrase that you cannot put in your own words, be sure to put it in quotations and, of course, cite the original source with page number(s).

While it is important to use a great deal of documentation from the literature that you have reviewed, and while you should cite every source, your paper should not be a kind of patchwork quilt with many patches and little quilting. Stringing together excerpts from someone else's writing and theorizing, even if properly cited, with little or no material of your own will result in a very poor, nonscholarly paper.

You may understand what literal plagiarism is—quoting directly from a source without citing where the information came from—but you also need to be aware of conceptual plagiarism. Conceptual plagiarism occurs when a writer presents someone else's original theories without crediting the source. In other words, if you write about the ego, the id, and the superego without alluding to Sigmund Freud as the originator of these concepts, you are engaging in conceptual plagiarism. While you will want to cite sources and use some excerpts directly from the readings you have reviewed, you must do this intelligently. Lifting entire sections off of the Internet, for example, even if one has properly cited them, is little more than thinly disguised plagiarism. Note that professors can easily use such tools as Turn It In at http://turnitin.com/static/index.html and iThenticate at http://www.ithenticate.com/static/home.html to verify that the content of your research paper is, in fact, original and that you did not plagiarize it from another source.

Remember also that, if you do not understand anything at all or very little about the theories or methodology in a particular article, you should not include that article in your literature review. Reporting on the article conveys the tacit assumption that you have understood its contents. Especially in upper-level undergraduate courses and in graduate school, orally defending in front of an individual or a committee a paper that has content that one does not fully understand can lead to a great deal of embarrassment (at best) and possibly a failing grade (at worst).

When you finally have your paper written, be sure to proofread it manually, as well as passing it through a spell-check program on your computer. Remember that a spell-check program will only find absolute misspellings. It will not detect incorrect grammar, errors in tenses, misspelled names of authors, and so on.

SHOULD WRITERS EXPRESS THEIR OWN OPINIONS?

Students will notice in much of what they read that the writing, even in a professional journal, seems to have a particular opinion or "bent" on their topic. Sometimes students ask if all scholarly writing should not be absolutely objective. We believe that "absolute objectivity" is an ideal that we have never seen in practice. For any social scientist to claim that he or she approaches a topic with no preconceptions, no prior-held beliefs, and no prejudices is, we believe, disingenuous. We have all lived in a world and formed a belief system. To assume that this will not influence our scientific research is to be less than candid with ourselves. We would even go further in stating that the most interesting writings are those that are forthright in stating their points of view.

What differentiates scientific writing from opinion papers, however, is the use of substantiation with research and data for one's point of view and the willingness to admit if one has found little support for one's hypothesis. Only if the writer feels passionately about a subject can the reader be expected to become enthused by a book or article.

SOME TIPS ON WRITING PAPERS AND SOME FREQUENT PITFALLS TO AVOID

1. *Do not use sexist language.* Instead of using the generic *he* or *his*, use sexually neutral language, such as *(s)he* or *his/her* or *his or her*. Students often argue that this will sound awkward or stilted. This kind of writing rarely sounds awkward or stilted, and, as more and more of the academic (and even popularized) literature is now written in this style, readers are becoming used to this phrasing. Be on your guard for sexist language where you might least expect it to crop up. For example, use the term *humankind* instead of *mankind* or *personnel* instead of *manpower*. You may also write in the plural third person (*they, their, them*).
2. *Do not use racist or ageist terms.* Once again, these terms may crop up more readily than one might imagine, and one must be vigilant. For example, one of us recently attended a workshop given by an academic in which he argued that, at his university, the administration wanted the faculty members to be "good little Indians." It took a great deal of persuading to convince this individual that he was indeed using racist language. Please also note that it is appropriate to refer to individuals under 18 years of age as *boys* or *girls* or *young men* or *young women*. Individuals over 18 years of age are referred to as *men* or *women*.
3. *Don't change verb tenses gratuitously.* Many writers shift back and forth between present tense and past tense. Writing in this way is both distracting and confusing.
4. *Always place modifying words as closely as possible to those words being modified.* Do not write, for example, "The president, who gave a speech in the pouring rain, out in the field in the middle of the afternoon, was profound." Rather, one might write, "The president was profound

in his speech given out in the pouring rain in the middle of the afternoon."

5. *Always write complete sentences.* Do not write informally and in the form of an outline. Many students write exactly as they would speak, that is, informally. This is not scholarly form and is truly unacceptable in a college-level paper. For your finished paper, phrases and shorthand are not acceptable at all.
6. *Do not use unnecessary commas, colons, and semicolons.* Students often think that when in doubt, use punctuation. Actually in this case, less is more. You should be sure that you are appropriately using any such punctuation.

Writers will look at a blank sheet of paper and wonder how it will be when their work is done. They often look at that sheet of paper for a very long time! Writing well does take time, in addition to a great deal of practice and hard work. Not only should the papers read well, they should look good too. We suggest that when reading the literature, you read with a writer's eye—recognize the writing style of the work; and when writing your paper, you write with a reader's eye—think about how well your readers will follow your work.

College campuses have writing centers that are available to students. Writing centers are places where students can go for help or simply work quietly knowing that assistance is nearby if needed. Questions may come up throughout the writing process. Mentors are often available to guide students through any aspect of the writing exercise, from understanding the assignment through reading final drafts. Students should never expect mentors to grade their papers. Nor should students expect mentors to be their editors. However, mentors do serve to help students each step of the way. We strongly encourage you to visit your campus writing center.

Professors are also available to help guide your work. If you are having difficulty at any point, seek out the professor. As always, it is best to come prepared to a meeting with your professor. Try not to be intimidated by the professors; after all, they have been where you are now and they want their students to do well.

You should begin the literature-gathering, note-taking, and organizing processes early so you may have ample time to write the paper. Putting a paper together is a constant work in progress. At some point you need to begin the writing process; at some point you must decide "This is the final version!" Do your best to make the reader want to read your paper.

8

Presenting the Research Paper

As part of your research assignment, you may be required to give a presentation. Students are often frightened of this because it involves standing and speaking before a group of people. Presenters who know their material and who have organized that material in a meaningful way are more likely to give interesting presentations to their fellow classmates. If you are giving a presentation to a class, then you should be prepared! A presentation is usually a somewhat simplified version of a more complex paper. You should do your best not to read a paper. However, you should have notes to follow and to guide you. In all cases, you should follow an outline. The guidelines for creating an outline are found in Chapter 4. Follow those steps in preparing your presentation.

Know your material! This is very important. While you may not refer to everything you know on your subject, knowledge allows you to confidently create a solid presentation. In addition, you may be asked questions that had not been addressed in the presentation. As someone who is expected to be familiar with a topic, you should be ready to answer many questions.

ENHANCING YOUR PRESENTATION: USING AUDIOVISUAL AIDS, COMPUTER-GENERATED GRAPHICS, OR A WEB PAGE

You may wish to enhance the presentation with audiovisual aids, computer-generated graphics, or a Web page. A multitude of audiovisual aids are available today. Most are quite simple to create and display. Even software-based audiovisuals are easy to design and use. Use audiovisual aids sparingly, however. They should not distract attention from the subject matter.

Audiovisual aids are used only to the extent that they enable you to convey information more clearly to your audience. These audiovisual aids should be used only as tools to make your presentation more comprehensible to your audience. These tools should not be used primarily to show that you have mastered this technology.

The following is a list of some audiovisual aids that you can use to make your presentation more interesting.

Transparencies

Probably the most simple to create, a transparency is a thin film of see-through plastic that enables light to pass through it. You can create any type of text or image on paper from which to make a transparency. Computer-generated graphics, hand-drawn images, and handwritten, typed, or word-processed text can be placed or printed on paper and a transparency made from that piece of paper. You can make your own transparencies in color or black and white. Office supply stores carry transparency sheets that you can feed into certain models of computer printers or through a photocopier. Copy centers on your campus or located in your area can make transparencies at low cost.

You will need an overhead projector to display your transparency on a screen for your audience to view. Check with your professor on the availability of an overhead projector at least 3–4 weeks prior to your presentation. Not all classrooms are equipped with overheads, and the professor may need to reserve one for you.

Visual Viewers

Sometimes referred to as an ELMO or a WolfVision Visualizer, a visual viewer is a piece of equipment that allows you to place any object on its platform and display it on a screen. The object can be a book, a page of text, or even a 3-D object. The viewer displays the object as it actually exists. Using a visual viewer can be very effective when showing an audience a section of text from a book, a color chart displaying data, a manuscript, and so on. Most viewers have the capability for you to enlarge the image. Like overhead projectors, not all classrooms are equipped with visual viewers. You may need to ask your professor to reserve one for you.

Computer-Generated Graphics

Software is available on most campuses to help you spruce up your presentation. Known as presentation software, these programs enable you to create "transparencies" on the computer and display them to your audience from the computer. In a few minutes you can create a visual program using presentation software. One such easy-to-learn program is called PowerPoint. For a more elaborate presentation, you may want to explore designing a multimedia program to show your audience. A multimedia program incorporates text, graphics, and sound and can include full-motion video. PowerPoint has the capabilities built within it for you to create a multimedia presentation.

Web Pages

Creating a Web page or even a simple Web site is very easy to do. The advantages of using a Web page in your presentation is that you can access Internet sites that you may want to show your audience as well as make the site available for your audience to access via the Internet after your presentation. Web pages provide you with much flexibility. You can create a PowerPoint presentation, provide links to quality Web sites, add sound and even video streaming for a complete multimedia experience. Many students now create Web sites on specific topics, make them available on the Web, then add the Internet address of the Web sites to their resumes so that potential employers can gain insight into the quality of work they can create. Software, such as DreamWeaver, is available that will guide you through the basics of creating a Web page or Web site. There are also books, such as Lynch and Horton's *Web Style Guide: Basic Design Principles for Creating Web Sites* (2001), that can assist you in developing an easy-to-navigate Web site.

If you decide to develop a Web page or Web site for your presentation, you will need to make sure that the room you are using for your presentation has a computer with the appropriate presentation and Web-browser software and the equipment to display the computer image on a screen. You will also need Internet access so that you can get to your Web site or page. It is a good idea to post your Web site on the Internet at least a few days prior to your presentation to make sure that it is accessible.

In addition to Web pages, multimedia presentations, and transparencies, you can also show video clips or clips from DVDs, music, or other sound recordings from MP3 players. Your information can be stored and accessed in a variety of ways, such as saving it to a computer disk, CD-ROM, USB port drive (which is the size of your thumbnail and can fit on a keychain), laptop computer, handheld PC, or Palm Pilot. Using any of these methods allows you to bring a large presentation to class on a small piece of equipment. Posting your presentation on the Web is also easy—as long as you have Internet access in the room you are presenting in.

Preplanning is strongly advised if you decide to use computer-generated graphics, multimedia, or the Web in your presentation, or if you decide to bring your presentation to class using any of the electronic devices listed above. You will need to check with your professor or computer center on your campus to determine the availability of computers, software, Internet access, and equipment to display your presentation. This should be done at least 3 to 4 weeks in advance of your presentation. You will also want to practice your presentation at least once in the room you will be using. This way, you can become familiar with the equipment lighting changes that you will need to make, and you will be assured that your program runs on the equipment provided. Do not count on developing your presentation at home and then using it successfully on campus without practicing. Computer hardware and software on campus may be incompatible with your home computer. It may seem like a waste of time, however, we have experienced presentations brought to class on a computer disk only to discover that the computer in the classroom only has a CD-ROM player and not a computer disk drive. Doing a rehearsal, or dry run, is essential.

DESIGNING EFFECTIVE VISUALS

You can follow these important tips when creating visual aids for your presentation. These suggestions will help make your presentation dynamic and interesting.

The Revealing Technique

We have found that the most effective visual aid presents no more than three or four statements or pieces of data or information at once. A good rule, whether using computer-generated screens or transparencies, is to use the "revealing" technique of presenting information to your audience. To do this, divide each page or screen into thirds. Present your data on the first third of the overhead, covering the second and third portions; continue by revealing the second portion, then third, until the entire screen is visible to the audience. Presenting all the information at once may overwhelm and confuse your audience. By revealing your information systematically, you keep your audience focused on the topic you are discussing.

Use of Color

When creating overheads using a color printer or computer-generated graphics program, consider using two or more colors to delineate different columns in a graphic or different threads of thought in a text presentation. In designing your presentation using computer presentation software such as PowerPoint, you can select various colors to highlight text and colors to diminish text you are not currently talking about. Color livens up your presentation for your audience.

Professional Presentations

Computer programs, such as Excel and PowerPoint, are widely available, which allows you to present data in a very professional-looking manner. You can develop bar graphs, pie charts, scattergrams, and even simple animation fairly easily. There are numerous options available for you to create visuals that are eye catching but that will also help your audience retain the information you present.

It would be nice if giving a presentation were not a high-anxiety event, as it is for many students. We do find, however, that the more concerned about presentations that students are, the more likely they are to be prepared. Keep in mind that your classmates are learning something from you. Know the material, have guidelines to follow, perhaps enhance the presentation, and be proud of your work. Throughout our lives we find we need to give presentations of one sort or another. There is no time like the present to begin!

Go to Worksheet 11: Presentation in Appendix C, and complete the questions.

9

Some Final Thoughts

A well-organized, well-written, and well-presented library research paper may seem overwhelming for most students at the beginning of the creative process. This manual provides step-by-step guidelines for students in the social sciences. The process should become less burdensome, if it is indeed a burden, with each paper that is written.

It should be clear by now that the process is quite tangible and explicit. Developing a research question is the first crucial step. Finding available material relating to the question requires both library skills and a critical analysis of the literature. The library is the main source of information. Once the material is sorted through, an outline is developed and the key points identified. At this point, it is extremely important to stay focused. Each key point in the outline must be expanded upon using the scholarly literature as the main source of information. In the final paper, sources must be properly cited. A complete reference list must be included.

While this all seems pro forma and routine, keep in mind that writing a library research paper for the social sciences involves a great deal of abstract thought, reflection, critical thinking, organization, and technical skill. These skills range from reading the research to writing and presenting the findings. Students should use any other available resources beyond this manual to help if there is a need. These resources include instructors, librarians, and campus writing centers.

Finally, in addition to enhancing one's knowledge on a topic and receiving a good class grade, writing a skillful library research paper and giving a successful presentation can be quite satisfying. The scholarly research, writing, and presentation processes provide students with a number of skills for life, such as the ability to view the world more objectively, understand and evaluate problems, understand personal problems in a broader social context, organize thoughts and information, conceptualize difficulties clearly, and write well. Thus, we encourage you to persevere. It is well worth the effort!

Appendix A: Research Questions Posed by Prior Students

Among the wide range of questions that could be posed by social sciences undergraduate students, the following issues have been researched by students we have worked with:

- Has education on AIDS in African American communities significantly helped to decrease the number of African Americans at risk for AIDS?
- What obstacles face young, single mothers and their children?
- Are children from divorced families more prone to delinquent activities than children from intact families?
- What is the relationship between marital status and workforce participation for women?
- How does access to contraceptives affect the likelihood that teenagers will use contraceptives?
- What is the relationship between socioeconomic factors and domestic violence?
- How does the level of education affect men's and women's perceptions of gender roles?
- How has the rise in bias-motivated crime against homosexual people in America during the last 30 years led to the development of legislation to address the issue of hate crimes based on sexual orientation?
- What is the relationship between neighborhood level of interaction and crime?
- How does smoking marijuana affect college students' academic performance?
- What is the affect of maternal employment on children's well-being?

- Is inner-city crime, especially that committed by young minorities, overrepresented in the media?
- Does the American news media depict youth violence in a fashion disproportionate to its coverage of violence as a whole?
- How does social support following an abusive childhood affect people's lives?
- How do women's work roles affect family life?
- How do grades in school influence deviance in later life?
- What factors influence people with terminal illness to choose euthanasia, specifically physician-assisted suicide?
- Does family structure affect a child's academic achievement?
- How do young women respond to the gender gap in wages?
- How do affirmative action policies, required by all companies, influence the hiring and placement of racial minorities and women?
- How closely linked are socioeconomic status during childhood and socioeconomic status in adulthood?
- How do preventative programs affect juvenile delinquency?
- How does drug use during adolescence affect identity formation?
- What is the relationship between teen substance abuse and teen physical violence in dating relationships?
- Have the educational requirements of occupations risen over the last 2 decades in a way that is consistent with the rewards of those occupations?
- Why is there an overrepresentation of minorities in the juvenile justice system?
- To what extent are women occupying executive-level management in the 500 (*Fortune 500*) public corporations?
- How does poverty affect children's success in school?
- Is there a difference in the number of cases of sexual aggression and sexual victimization between schools with and without rape prevention or education programs?
- Does pornography influence negative attitudes toward women?
- How does after-school care affect adolescents' drinking and school performance?
- How does being in college influence drinking behavior?

Appendix B: Example Paper

Please note: The numbering of paragraphs that follow in the example paper is for instructional purposes only. Numbering paragraphs is not acceptable APA format. Do not number the paragraphs when writing your paper. Use 1-inch margins on the top and bottom of each page. For the first page only, start typing 2 inches from the top of the page.

Double space the text of your paper. Do not use excessively large or small font size. Our suggestion is for you to use a font similar to our examples in this text.

Include a title page for your paper. Follow our example. The title should be your research question.

Staple your paper in the upper left-hand corner with one staple prior to turning it in to your professor.

Is Violence in Dating Relationships
Conceptually Distinct From Violence in Marital Relationships?

Class Name
Time Class Meets
Date
Instructor's Name
Your Name

Paragraph 1 The purpose of this paper is to examine physical violence in dating relationships. Specifically, this paper addresses the question Is violence in dating relationships conceptually distinct from violence in marital relationships? The following factors are taken into consideration. First, dating violence is described as a form of family violence or, more precisely, intimate violence. Second, the role of dating and courtship must be taken into account. Third, dating violence is recognized as being distinct yet on a continuum of other forms of violence.

Paragraph 2 Dating violence is a form of family violence. Research in the area of family violence had it beginnings in the late 1960s and early 1970s. In 1985, the second national survey of family violence was conducted by the Family Violence Research Laboratory at the University of New Hampshire (Straus & Gelles, 1990). The rate of violence against children was 23/1,000 (1.5 million children each year) when socially sanctioned acts of slapping or hitting with an object are omitted. It increased to 110/1,000 (6.9 million children each year) when all acts of violence were included.

Paragraph 3 Straus and Gelles (1990) found in the 1985 National Family Violence Survey that about 161 couples per 1,000 couples experienced one or more physical assaults on a partner during that year and that 34/1,000 wives were severely assaulted (1.8 million) by their husbands. Severe assaults involved the most dangerous acts, such as punching, biting, kicking, and choking. The Family Violence Research Laboratory studies used the Conflict Tactics Scale to measure the frequency of self-reported incidents of how persons deal with conflict in their relationships, from reasoning, threatening, or using force. The conflict tactics scale is used regularly in studies to determine frequency and occurrences of violence in relationships.

Paragraph 4 Researchers are now examining violence by women toward men. Early studies by Steinmetz (1977–1978) and Straus and Gelles (1990) showed that women were violent toward men. These studies received criticism in the family violence research world, particularly from feminist researchers who were focusing on women as victims and men as perpetrators as a result of inequality. For example, Irene Frieze (2000) explained that feminist researchers assumed that men were aggressors and women victims of marital violence. Other actors had to be considered as well to help understand violence in families and in other types of intimate relationships that do not limit the theoretical focus to male domination and female subordination (e.g., see Stets & Pirog-Good, 1989). This is most clear in efforts to understand violence within gay and lesbian relationships (Letellier, 1994; Lobel, 1986; Renzetti, 1994).

Paragraph 5 Research in the family violence area increasingly shows that women can be, and are, violent toward men. Once again quoting Irene Frieze (2000), "for feminist researchers of battered wives, one of the most disconcerting findings of studies of dating violence was that young women were found to be at least as violent, if not more violent than, the young men they were dating" (para. 8).

Paragraph 6 In the United States, romantic love emerges in the context of dating. Dating is a form of mate selection that involves the least commitment between couples. Teenagers are learning how to deal with each other as well as adjusting to physical sexual maturity. This can be a traumatic period. Some people are afraid of intimacy because it makes them more vulnerable; for example, they do not want to be dependent upon someone else or risk being hurt. Irene Frieze (2000) wrote a chronology of the research on family violence and stated about dating violence "although researchers continued to study marital violence, other social scientists were investigating another form of male–female violence—dating violence. Researchers came to believe that a pattern of violence was often established before marriage, during the dating period" (para. 8). James, West, Deters, and Armijo (2000) argued that dating violence among adolescents is a serious health problem that needs to be addressed.

Paragraph 7 It is becoming increasingly evident that violence is not limited to persons who are related to each other either legally or biologically. What was once thought of as a rare occurrence between family members (Gelles, 1980) is now recognized as a common, often socially accepted phenomenon in many, if not all, types of intimate relationships. James

Makepeace (1981) was the first to suggest that social scientists examine courtship violence as a link between violence experienced in childhood and later violence experienced in marriage. Others suggested that relationship violence be examined regardless of marital status because abuse in courtship resembles that which is reported in marriage (Roscoe & Benaske, 1985).

Paragraph 8 Makepeace initially hypothesized in 1981 that abusive relationships would terminate for dating couples more quickly than in marital relationships because the couples' reasons for staying together in marriage did not seem to apply in dating relationships. Twenty-one percent of the respondents in his college survey had at least one direct experience with courtship violence. The forms of violence most often sustained were pushing and slapping, while more severe forms of violence were sustained least often, such as punching, striking with an object, assaulting with a weapon, or choking. Contrary to his expectations, abusive relationships between dating partners did not result in relationship termination following physically violent arguments more quickly than between married partners. Other studies have found high percentages of physical violence in dating relationships. Early studies showed that 20 to 66% of couples experienced some form of violence (Laner & Thompson, 1982; McKinney, 1986; Pagelow, 1984). Those figures appear to be consistent with more recent research (Frieze, 2005).

Paragraph 9 Henton, Cate, Koval, Lloyd, and Christopher (1983) carried out the first study of dating violence among high school youth. They found that 12% of high school students had experienced violence in dating relationships. Current studies of dating violence among high school students, for example by James et al. (2000), found rates of 19 to 59% had been the victim of physical violence. James et al. (2000) studied psychological and physical abuse in a sample of adolescents. Their findings reinforced that at least 25% of adolescents experience psychological and physical abuse in their relationships. They defined youth violence in dating relationships as a serious public health problem that needs to be addressed.

Paragraph 10 Another study carried out by Howard and Wang (2003) used survey data from the 1999 Youth Risk Behavior Survey to identify risk profiles of adolescent girls who were victims of dating violence. The survey sample was a representative sample of 9th- through 12th-grade U.S. females (N = 7,824). They found that almost 1 in 10 of them reported being a victim of physical dating violence within the past year. Researchers are examining dating violence and its relationship to high-risk behaviors, such as substance abuse, feelings of sadness or hopelessness, and thoughts of suicide.

Paragraph 11 The research on dating violence is being used in ways to help stop the violence and protect victims of violence. With access to information on the computer readily available, prevention programs are easily accessible. One search on Yahoo! under *dating violence* came up with 1,280,000 results (Yahoo! Search, 2005). The information on dating violence is often a part of a larger Web site on domestic violence or crime victimization. For instance, the Alabama Coalition Against Domestic Violence (ACADV, n.d.) is a "nonprofit organization dedicated to working toward a peaceful society where domestic violence no longer exists" (para. 1). The categories linked on the site are abusers, barriers, children, dating, facts, friends, legal, links, safety, shelters, and stories. Under "dating," users are given a definition of *dating violence*, statistics on dating violence, guidelines for developing a dating safety plan, and a dating bill of rights, which is broken down into individual rights and responsibility toward others.

Paragraph 12 The research on dating violence and other forms of family violence is vast. Stets and Straus (1990) questioned the notion that the marriage license is a hitting license if violent incidents occur in intimate relationships outside of marriage to the extent that they do. While researchers initially thought that violence between intimate others was confined to marriage, they now know this is not the case. In general, research on dating violence is studied as a distinct phenomenon but is increasingly examined in the broader context of intimate violence.

Reference List

Alabama Coalition Against Domestic Violence. (n.d.). Retrieved December 26, 2004, from http://www.acadv.org/about.html

Frieze, I. H. (2000). Violence in close relationships—development of a research area: Comment on Archer (2000). *Psychological Bulletin, 126*(5), 681–684.

Frieze, I. H. (2005). *Hurting the one you love: Violence in relationships.* Belmont, CA: Wadsworth.

Gelles, R. (1980). Violence in the family: A review of research in the seventies. *Journal of Marriage and the Family, 43*(4), 878–885.

Henton, J., Cate, R., Koval, J, Lloyd, S., & Christopher, F. (1983). Romance and violence in dating relationships. *Journal of Family Issues, 4*, 467–482.

Howard, D. E., & Wang, M. Q. (2003). Risk profiles of adolescent girls who were victims of dating violence. *Adolescence, 38*(149), 1–14.

James, W. H., West, C., Deters, K. E., & Armijo, E. (2000). Youth dating violence. *Adolescence, 35*(139), 455–465.

Laner, M. R., & Thompson, J. (1982). Abuse and aggression in courting couples. *Deviant Behavior, 3*, 228–244.

Letellier, P. (1994). Gay and bisexual male domestic violence victimization: Challenges to feminist theory and responses to violence. *Violence and Victims, 9*, 96–106.

Lobel, K. (Ed.). (1986). *Naming the violence: Speaking out about lesbian battering.* Seattle, WA: The Seal Press.

Makepeace, J. M. (1981). Courtship violence among college students. *Family Relations, 30*(1), 97–101.

McKinney, K. (1986). Perceptions of courtship violence: Gender difference and involvement. *Free Inquiry Into Creative Sociology, 14*, 55–60.

Pagelow, M. D. (1984). *Family violence.* New York: Praeger.

Renzetti, C. M. (1994). On dancing with a bear: Reflections on some of the current debates among domestic violence theorists. *Violence and Victims, 9*, 195–200.

Roscoe, B., & Benaske, N. (1985, July). Courtship violence experienced by abused wives: Similarities in patterns of abuse. *Family Relations, 34*(3), 419–424.

Steinmetz, S. K. (1977–1978). The battered husband syndrome. *Victimology, 2*, 499–509.

Stets, J. E., & Pirog-Good, M. A. (1989). Patterns of physical and sexual abuse for men and women in dating relationships: A descriptive analysis. *Journal of Family Violence, 4*(1), 67–76.

Stets, J. E., & Straus, M. A. (1990). The marriage license as a hitting license: A comparison of assaults in dating, cohabiting, and married couples. In M. A. Straus & R. J. Gelles (Eds.). *Physical violence in American families: Risk factors and adaptations to violence in 8,145 families* (pp. 227–244). New Brunswick, NJ: Transaction Books.

Straus, M. A., & Gelles, R. J. (1990). How violent are American families? Estimates from the national family violence resurvey and other studies. In M. A. Straus & R. J. Gelles (Eds.). *Physical violence in American families: Risk factors and adaptations to violence in 8,145 families* (pp. 95–112). New Brunswick, NJ: Transaction Books.

Yahoo! Search. (n.d.). *Dating violence*. Retrieved January 4, 2005, from http://search.yahoo.com/search?p=Dating+Violence

Appendix C: Worksheets

In this appendix you will find 11 worksheets that will guide you through the research and writing process. This is the list of worksheet numbers and their titles:

Worksheet	Title
1	Selecting a Topic
2	Narrowing and Focusing Your Topic
3	Scholarly vs. Popular Literature
4	Best Places for Information
5	Your Research Strategy
6	Locating Books
7	Chapters in Books
8	Locating Scholarly Articles
9	Evaluating Internet Information
10	Outlining the Research Paper
11	Presentation

WORKSHEET 1:
SELECTING A TOPIC

Name: ______________________________ Date: ______________

The purpose of this exercise is to brainstorm topics you are interested in writing your paper on.

1. Write down three ideas you have for your paper. Select topics that are of interest to you and meet the guidelines your professor has set for the course.

Topic 1:

Topic 2:

Topic 3:

2. Select the *one* topic you are most interested in writing about. Why are you interested in exploring this topic?

3. What do you already know about this topic?

4. Using this topic, decide which discipline you will use in approaching the topic. For example, will you approach this topic from a sociological point of view, a psychological point of view, a criminal justice point of view, etc.?

5. From this topic, develop three possible research questions you might explore.

Research Question 1:

Research Question 2:

Research Question 3:

WORKSHEET 2: NARROWING AND FOCUSING YOUR TOPIC

Name: ____________________________ Date: ______________

The purpose of this exercise is to develop a refined search question or statement.

1. What is the topic you wish to research (as you selected in Worksheet 1)?

2. What will be the time period of your research (e.g., last 5 years, last 2 decades, 1900s, comparing 2 decades [1960s and 1990s], etc.)?

3. What is the geographic area you are interested in exploring within this topic (e.g., United States, comparing two states [e.g., California and New York], a specific region [southeast], comparing two countries [e.g., Australia and Japan])?

4. What population or group will you be focusing on (e.g., men, women, children, adults, teenagers, the elderly, Irish, Scottish, African American, Spanish, etc.)? Be as specific as possible.

5. What aspects or viewpoints will you focus on, as you determined in Worksheet 1 (sociological, economic, medical, etc.)? Remember, your research can be cross-disciplinary.

6. Taking the information from steps 1 through 5, write your topic in the form of a more refined research question or statement (e.g., What is the relationship between sex role attitudes and work aspirations of adolescent girls and boys in the United States, comparing the 1960s to the 2000s?).

WORKSHEET 3: SCHOLARLY VS. POPULAR LITERATURE

Name: ______________________________ Date: _______________

The purpose of this exercise is to identify the differences between articles published in scholarly journals and those published in popular magazines.

1. Go to the library and find one issue of a scholarly journal and one issue of a popular magazine. Examples of scholarly journals are *American Journal of Sociology, Journal of the American Medical Association,* and *Journal of Criminal Justice.* Examples of popular magazines are *Newsweek, Time,* and *U.S. News and World Report.*
2. Using the Table 2.1 in Chapter 2, compare the two publications and complete the following chart. You may select one article from each publication to answer the questions in the chart.

	Scholarly Journal	Popular Magazine
Title of Publication		
Date of Issue		
Advertisements Included?		
Length (in Pages) of Article?		
Author(s) Given?		
Author(s) Credentials?		
References Given?		
Photographs Included?		
Other Differences:		

WORKSHEET 4:
BEST PLACES FOR INFORMATION

Name: ______________________________ Date: ______________

The purpose of this exercise is to determine what kind of information you need and to identify the best places to look for information on your topic.

1. Using your topic, check the kind of information you need for your research. Keep in mind course requirements (e.g., Does your professor want you to read scholarly articles as opposed to popular magazine articles?).

Your research question or statement:

Kind of Information Needed:

Reference books (encyclopedias, dictionaries, etc.)
Chapters in books
Popular magazine articles
Scholarly journal articles
Internet sites
Videos (documentaries)
Interviews
Statistics
Other: ____________________________________

2. Check the best places to look for the information you need. (Check all that apply.)

Reference collection in library for encyclopedias, dictionaries, etc.
Online public access catalog (library's card catalog on computer for books, videos, etc.)
Browsing the library's book collection in selected LC Classification section(s) (e.g., BF, H, and R)
Searching computer indexes for journal articles (e.g., *Social Sciences Index*)
Searching the Internet

WORKSHEET 5: YOUR RESEARCH STRATEGY

Name: ______________________________ Date: ______________

1. State your topic as completely as you can:

2. Circle two or three of the most important keywords.

3. Write each key word you circled in step 2 in the space below, then list related terms (synonyms), if applicable.

Keyword	Synonym
a. ________________	________________
________________	________________
b. ________________	________________
________________	________________
c. ________________	________________
________________	________________
d. ________________	________________
________________	________________

4. Write down any scholars' or experts' names on the topic that is being researched. If you do not know of any names, that is OK. Try checking your textbook or specialized encyclopedia on your topic for names of scholars who have researched your topic. You can then search for information about your topic by typing scholars' names into computer databases and on the Internet.

You can now use the information on this worksheet to search various computer databases and print sources for information on your research question.

WORKSHEET 6: LOCATING BOOKS

Name: ________________________________ Date: ______________

The purpose of this exercise is to locate two books on your chosen topic.

1. Search your library's online public access catalog by subject or keyword (either by visiting the library or searching the library's catalog via the Internet, if available).
2. Locate two books on your topic. Write down the information for each book below, or print off the information from the library's catalog and attach it to this assignment with a staple.

Book 1
Author(s):
Title:
Date:
Place of publication (If more than one city is listed, select the city located closest to your home in the country you reside.):
Publisher:
Call number:

Book 2
Author(s):
Title:
Date:
Place of publication:
Publisher:
Call number:

WORKSHEET 7: CHAPTERS IN BOOKS

Name: ______________________________ Date: ______________

The purpose of this worksheet is to enable you to obtain all information needed to correctly cite information taken from a chapter in a book. Select one book you have located on your topic. Then select a chapter out of the book and complete the worksheet.

Author(s) of the chapter:
Title of the chapter:
Date:
Editor(s) of the book (if the book is edited):
Title of the book:
Page numbers of the chapter:
Place of publication:
Publisher:

WORKSHEET 8: LOCATING SCHOLARLY ARTICLES

Name: ______________________________ Date: ______________

The purpose of this exercise is to locate two scholarly journal articles on your chosen topic.

1. Search a computer or print index for two scholarly articles on your topic. Search by subject or keyword (search the index, such as the index, either by visiting the library or searching the library's catalog via the Internet, if available).
2. Locate two scholarly journal articles on your topic. Write down the information for each article below, or print off the information and attach it to this assignment with a staple.

Article 1
Author(s):
Article title:
Journal title:
Issue date:
Volume:
Number:
Pages:

Article 2
Author(s):
Article title:
Journal title:
Issue date:
Volume:
Number:
Pages:

3. What index did you search to locate these articles?

WORKSHEET 9: EVALUATING INTERNET INFORMATION

Name: ______________________________ Date: ______________

The purpose of this exercise is to locate and evaluate an Internet site related to your topic.

1. What is your research question or statement?

2. What search engine(s) did you use?

   Google (http://www.google.com)
   HOTBOT (http://www.hotbot.com)
   Yahoo (http://www.yahoo.com)
   Other:

3. What subject(s) did you type in for your search?

4. How many Web sites ("records" or "hits") did you retrieve?

5. Click on one Web site and go to it.

What is the Web address? http://____________________
What is the name of the Web site?

What is the purpose of the Web site?

What kind of information is included in the Web site? (Check all that apply.)

Advertising
Articles
Graphics (pictures)
Maps
Statistics
Other information:

Who are the author(s) of the Web site?

What are the author(s) credentials (M.D., Ph.D., etc.)?

What organization or institution are the authors affiliated with (college, university, etc.)?

When was the Web site last updated?

How would this information be useful to you? If the information is not useful, why not?

Print off the first page of the information from the Web site you are interested in and attach it to this assignment with a staple.

WORKSHEET 10:
OUTLINING THE RESEARCH PAPER

Name: ______________________________ Date: ______________

The purpose of this worksheet is to develop an outline for your research paper. You will then be able to use this worksheet to develop an organized research paper.

1. State your research question.

2. Complete this section of the worksheet by writing down three key points you will cover in your paper. Under each key point, write down three subpoints that support the main key point.

Key Point 1 and subpoints to be addressed in paper:
  a.
  b.
  c.

Key Point 2 and subpoints to the addressed in paper:
  a.
  b.
  c.

Key Point 3 and subpoints to be addressed in paper:
  a.
  b.
  c.

3. Write down any notes that may be useful in completing your paper.

4. Write a draft of your concluding paragraph here.

5. List your references cited in your paper, using the appropriate style (e.g., APA style) here.

WORKSHEET 11: PRESENTATION

Name: ______________________________ Date: ______________

The purpose of this worksheet is to outline your presentation.

1. State your research question.

2. As you did in Worksheet 10, develop three key points and subpoints that you will cover in your presentation.

Key Point 1 and subpoints to be addressed in presentation:
   a.
   b.
   c.

Key Point 2 and subpoints to be addressed in presentation:
   a.
   b.
   c.

Key Point 3 and subpoints to be addressed in presentation:
   a.
   b.
   c.

3. Write down any notes that may help you in your presentation.

4. Write a draft of your concluding paragraph for your presentation.

5. List the references that you will be citing in your presentation following a specific style, such as APA style. It is always a good idea to provide your audience with a handout listing the information you cited. In this way, the audience can read further on your topic.

6. Make a list of audiovisual aids that you will be using in your presentation.

Appendix D: Blank Citation Forms

This appendix contains blank citation forms. Use the forms to record complete information about the sources you may cite in your paper. Forms contained in this appendix are for citing books, scholarly articles, chapters in books, and Internet sites.

When you complete the forms, cut the pages and place them in alphabetical order by first author's last name to create your reference list. If no author appears for a citation, place the citation in order alphabetically by title. If there is more than one year listed, select the most recent. Please note that when citing the city of a publication, select the city within your country that is closest to you geographically. For example, for a book with the following cities listed: Toronto, Canada; New York; and San Francisco, California, if you are located in Buffalo, New York, you would list New York as the city of publication.

BOOK REFERENCES

Author(s):

Title of book:

Year of publication:

City of publication:

Publishing company:

Author(s):

Title of book:

Year of publication:

City of publication:

Publishing company:

Author(s):

Title of book:

Year of publication:

City of publication:

Publishing company:

Author(s):

Title of book:

Year of publication:

City of publication:

Publishing company:

CHAPTERS IN BOOKS REFERENCES

Author(s) of chapter:

Title of chapter:

Year of publication:

Editor(s) of book (if any):

Title of book:

Page numbers of chapter:

City of publication:

Publishing company:

Author(s) of chapter:

Title of chapter:

Year of publication:

Editor(s) of book (if any):

Title of book:

Page numbers of chapter:

City of publication:

Publishing company:

Author(s) of chapter:

Title of chapter:

Year of publication:

Editor(s) of book (if any):

Title of book:

Page numbers of chapter:

City of publication:

Publishing company:

JOURNAL ARTICLE REFERENCES

Author(s):

Title of article:

Year of publication:

Journal name:

Volume number:

Issue number:

Page numbers of article:

Author(s):

Title of article:

Year of publication:

Journal name:

Volume number:

Issue number:

Page numbers of article:

Author(s):

Title of article:

Year of publication:

Journal name:

Volume number:

Issue number:

Page numbers of article:

INTERNET REFERENCES

Author(s) of article:

Name of article:

Date site/article was created:

Name of site (if different from article):

Author(s) of site (if different from article):

Date you accessed the site:

URL (http://) address or database:

Author(s) of article:

Name of article:

Date site/article was created:

Name of site (if different from article):

Author(s) of site (if different from article):

Date you accessed the site:

URL (http://) address or database:

Author(s) of article:

Name of article:

Date site/article was created:

Name of site (if different from article):

Author(s) of site (if different from article):

Date you accessed the site:

URL (http://) address or database:

Bibliography

Borgatta, E. F., & Montgomery, R. J. (Eds.). (2000). *Encyclopedia of sociology*. New York: Macmillan.

Cook, K. N., Kunkel, L. R., & Weaver, S. M. (1995). Cooperative learning in bibliographic instruction. *Research Strategies, 13*, 17–25.

Diagnostic and statistical manual of mental disorders: DSM-IV-TR (Text Revision) (4th ed.). (2000). Washington, DC: American Psychiatric Association.

The encyclopedia of social psychology. (1996). Oxford: Basil Blackwell.

Kuper, A., & Kuper, J. (Eds.). (2005). *The social science encyclopedia*. New York: Routledge.

Levinson, D. (Ed.). (1995). *Encyclopedia of marriage and the family*. New York: Macmillan.

Lynch, P. J., & Horton, S. (2001). *Web style guide: Basic design principles for creating Web sites.* New Haven, CT: Yale University Press.

Maddox, G. L. (Ed.). (2001). *Encyclopedia of aging*. New York: Springer.

Magill, F. N. (Ed.). (1994). *Survey of social science.* Englewood Cliffs, NJ: Salem Press.

Meehl, P. E. (1960). The cognitive activity of the clinician. *American Psychologist, 15*, 19–27.

Physicians' desk reference: Guide to drug interactions, side effects, indications. (1992–1996). Montvale, NJ: Medical Economics Data.

Piotrowski, N. A. (Ed.). (2003). *Magill's encyclopedia of social science: Psychology*. Hackensack, NJ: Salem Press.

Ponzetti, J. (Ed.). (2003). *International encyclopedia of marriage and the family*. New York: Macmillan Reference USA.

Publication manual of the American Psychological Association (5th ed.). (2002). Washington, DC: American Psychological Association.

Sproull, N. L. (1995). *Handbook of research methods: A guide for practitioners and students in the social sciences* (2nd ed.). Lanham, MD: Scarecrow Press.

Stearns, P. N. (Ed.). (1994). *Encyclopedia of social history*. New York: Garland Press.

Steffens, H. J., & Dickerson, M. J. (1987). *Writer's guide.* Lexington, MA: D. C. Heath.

Index

About the Authors

Gail M. Staines, Ph.D., is assistant provost for University Libraries at Saint Louis University in St. Louis, Missouri. Prior to this appointment, Gail served as executive director of the Western New York Library Resources Council. She holds an M.L.S. and a doctorate in higher education administration with an emphasis in academic librarianship from the University at Buffalo and served as visiting professor in the Department of Library and Information Studies, School of Informatics, at the University at Buffalo. An author of several publications and a frequent presenter at state and national conferences, Gail's primary areas of research are information literacy, management, and leadership. She was selected as one of *Library Journal*'s Movers and Shakers in 2004.

Katherine Johnson, Ph.D., is professor of sociology at Niagara County Community College in western New York State. She has conducted research in the area of domestic violence, with a focus on dating violence and sexual abuse. Currently, her research focus is in urban studies. As an urban sociologist, she is studying a local movement of concerned community citizens and community leaders in their efforts to overcome years of urban decline. Her focal point centers on the adaptive reuse of an old high school as an arts and cultural center in a city that has suffered the long-term effects of deindustrialization.

Mark Bonacci, Ph.D., is professor of human services at Niagara County Community College. Mark holds a B.A. in psychology from Manhattanville College, an M.S.W. from New York University, and a Ph.D. in psychology from the University at Buffalo. He teaches such courses as Introduction to Human Services, Introduction to Addictions: The Individual and the Family, Human Services Research and Synthesis, Substance Abuse Interventions, Chemical Dependency Topics, Introduction to Psychology, Developmental Psychology: A Lifespan Approach, and Social Psychology. Mark has a strong interest in supporting those with HIV/AIDS.